S0-BHS-559

UNCONDITIONAL LOVE and FORGIVENESS

Edith R. Stauffer, Ph.D.

Foreword by Robert A. Anderson, M.D.

UNCONDITIONAL LOVE AND FORGIVENESS

Edith R. Stauffer, Ph.D.

Triangle Publishers

Distributed by
Psychosynthesis International
Post Office Box 926
Diamond Springs, California 95619

Copyright © 1987 by Edith R. Stauffer, Ph.D.

All rights reserved. No part of this book may be reproduced or transmitted in any form by any means, including photocopying, recording, or any information storage or retrieval system, except as expressly permitted in the 1976 Copyright Act or in writing by the Publisher.

First printing: January 1987
Second printing: July, 1988

Typeset by MRB, Typographer, Glendale, California.

Manufactured in the United States of America by
BookCrafters
Chelsea, Michigan

ISBN: 0-940111-03-9

DEDICATION

This book is dedicated to all those who want to be whole in their physical bodies; to have loving, accepting relationships; to experience the transpersonal qualities of serenity, peace, joy, humor, understanding, forgiveness, compassion, and unconditional love; to be in harmony with their environment; to serve humanity and create a peaceful world.

CONTENTS

PART THREE

ACKNOWLEDGMENTS

I wish to thank and express my gratitude to all the many who have helped me to write this book, especially those I had a need to forgive. It was through some of them I learned the relief and benefit of unconditional love and forgiveness.

This book has been a long transformational process. I am grateful to have learned some of the great Laws of Life through writing it and living it.

I appreciate the encouragement, inspiration and wisdom of my friend and teacher, Roberto Assagioli, with whom I had the privilege of studying in 1968, 1972, and 1973. He lived what he taught. The principles of psychosynthesis are woven into the fabric of this book.

I'm grateful to my teacher and friend, Dan MacDougald, for introducing me to the life-changing qualities of the Aramaic language and for giving me the book, *Enlightenment*, passages from an ancient Syriac New Testament scribed in Aramaic. I have appreciated his encouraging me to write this book. His wisdom of how the mind functions has been a most valuable contribution.

I thank Ira Rifkin for urging me to write stories of the people who have changed their lives through unconditional love and forgiveness and for his patience and expertise in teaching me how to do it. (All case names mentioned in this book are false, although their stories are true.)

Joann and Robert Anderson gave considerable time, guidance, and encouragement as the manuscript developed, for which I'm grateful.

Appreciation is extended to Merrie Smith and Suzanne Mikesell for their ability to edit my writing and for making clear what I want to say to you in this book.

A special thanks to Elly Victoria Darwin for her midwifing this book through the computer and reminding me of all the many things to do next.

The cover design was perfected by Tim Waldner, to whom I give thanks.

I thank Shirley Perry for providing the illustrations throughout the book and also for the many hours of manuscript typing.

I deeply appreciate the consultation and guidance on production matters given by my grandson, Craig Evans.

It is with deep gratitude and appreciation that I acknowledge each of my readers, reviewers, clients, students, and those who have attended my hundreds of workshops in various parts of the world. You have given me the zeal to learn that the laws in this book work every time. You have been wonderful teachers for me in learning the dynamic process of forgiveness.

To my husband, Paul, for his love, support, and patience—as I have given him many opportunities to practice forgiveness—I say thank you.

Edith R. Stauffer, Ph.D.
Diamond Springs, California
1987

FOREWORD

The material covered in this book fills a void in the repertoire of thoughtful practitioners, therapists, and religious counselors who see their patients, clients, and parishoners as whole beings. The content goes beyond the bounds of traditional psychological approaches; in many ways it is a map for the never-never land between psychosomatic medicine, theology and religious belief systems, and psychotherapy.

The reason for including attitudes as important subjects for action by therapists, and as serious consideration for clients who desire to grow, can be seen by looking at the function of the attitudes themselves. Attitudes determine the quality of our perceptions. Since we think, feel, act, and process information based not on reality, but rather on our *perception* of reality (the two are not the same), it is essential to consider our attitude or mind set.[1]

The evolution of attitudes as subjects for scientific research has been apparent for the past two decades. In 1968 Wolff said, "Of crucial importance is the need for every [person] to understand with full appreciation the truly poisonous nature of hate, resentment, jealousy, frustration, envy and fear."[2] How predictively true this insight has proved to be!

A prospective study was conducted of medical students, following them as physicians for twenty-five years. A hostility scale was constructed from a special adaptation of the Minnesota Multiphasic Personality Inventory (MMPI). It showed that the incidence of heart attacks was 4.4-fold greater for the high-hostility group than the low-hostility group. The total mortality for the same high-hostility subjects was 6.6-fold greater than the low-hostility group over the same twenty-five-year period.[3] Hostility, as the prototypical negative attitude, is plainly associated with significantly greater mortality and disease.

The need for a set of positive attitudes from which to operate is patently apparent from these studies. The eight transpersonal attitudes highlighted by Edith Stauffer, including unconditional love and forgiveness, are the prototype for the positive attitudes which are increasingly being linked to greater health, joy, creativity, and self-actualization.

Rewarding change is rarely the result of the chance association of random events. Over the last three decades the recall of the will from the forgotten realms of therapeutic antiquity has been an exciting development. The evolution of thought surrounding the concept of an inner self around which the personality elements become organized has provided the framework for understanding the use of the will in therapy. The will, as a prime function of the inner self, has the power to evoke changes and institute growth—sometimes quite dramatic—within the personality structure. The exciting client stories with which Edith Stauffer has punctuated this volume are the evidence of the importance of utilizing the will for unconditional love and forgiveness.

The bonding of the self, as the center of the personality, with the Naphsha, the timeless center of our infinite existence, makes the exciting leap toward wholeness nearly complete. Understanding the influence of the Infinite Source, or God, on the Naphsha elevates the enthusiasm of our search for wholeness to a sense of completeness.

Change occurs at many levels. The change which evolves from incorporating love and forgiveness is profound. It is a quantum leap into the journey of our highest fulfillment. It is a candle lighting the void of our previous lack of understanding.

Therapists, physicians, health practitioners, counselors, and those in religious service will find the principles of *Unconditional Love and Forgiveness* of great personal and professional use, as have I. The non-professional reader will find the content and exercises applicable at every level of understanding.

Reading *Unconditional Love and Forgiveness* is like coming home; it is where we truly belong.

Robert A. Anderson, M.D., has practiced family medicine for twenty-six years. He is a Diplomate of the American Board of Family Practice, a charter fellow of the American Academy of Family Physicians, and Clinical Assistant Professor of Family Medicine at the University of Washington in Seattle. He is President of the American Holistic Medical Association and is a certified Psychosynthesist.

Part
One

Chapter 1
INTRODUCTION

Unconditional Love and Forgiveness is based on the principles of two bodies of work: the ancient Essene *Code of Conduct,* written in the Aramaic language and painstakingly rendered into appropriate English by Sadook de Mar Shimun;[1] and psychosynthesis, a holistic, transpersonal psychology created by Roberto Assagioli, M.D.[2] I have integrated and synthesized fifteen years of research, study, and personal application of the Essene laws with twenty-five years of psychosynthesis study. These two approaches to life and personal development are the most dynamic, creative, time-saving, and life-changing I have known in my thirty-five years of psychological training and counseling.

I first learned about the Essenes—members of an ancient sect who lived three centuries before and one century after Christ—in 1970. Dan MacDougald, an Atlanta lawyer, was teaching Georgia State Prison inmates a course he'd written called "Emotional Maturity Instruction,"[3] based on the Essene *Code of Conduct.* Sixty-five percent of the incarcerated offenders in his course returned to normal civilian life as law-abiding citizens upon release from prison. The training they received consisted of thirty hours of study and practice over a period of fifteen weeks.

Frank Goble, Director of the Thomas Jefferson Research Foundation, and I brought Mr. MacDougald to Los Angeles to give three weeks of instruction to twenty psychologists. As a member of that group I was trained in the Essene laws. I continue to study and practice them to this day.

I also had the good fortune to study psychosynthesis with its founder, the late Roberto Assagioli, at the Psychosynthesis Institute in Florence, Italy. Dr. Assagioli brought together Western psychology and Eastern tradition into a psychology that unifies all aspects of the person— physical, emotional, mental, and spiritual. From 1910-1964 Assagioli developed the principles and methods of psychosynthesis used today in psychotherapy, education, business, medicine, music, and healing.

The Essene *Code of Conduct,* written so many centuries ago, describes what many therapists and individuals are finding in transpersonal psychology today, and what I found in my work with Assagioli in the mid '70s. The Code's Law of Attitudes (presented in Part Two) superbly conveys the concepts of transpersonal consciousness. The Code and psychosynthesis both have to do with raising consciousness above the illusion most of us experience—that of seeing ourselves as separate from others. Both emphasize the creative use of the will and the utilization of transpersonal levels of awareness for maintaining and increasing personal health and universal harmony.

Ancient Beginnings of
Transpersonal Psychology

The Dead Sea Scrolls, discovered in 1945, have shed much light on the Essenes, how they lived, their values, their great contributions to our spiritual traditions. They were known for their ability to heal and to live harmonious lives in their community at a time when war and strife prevailed. They searched the scriptures daily and kept the laws, brought forth in their Code, which taught them how to relate to life, to all people, and to the Source—God.

The Essenes expressed an exceptional knowledge of psychology in their practice of communion with natural and cosmic forces. They understood both the subconscious and the conscious mind and were well aware of the power of each.

The first activity of their day was a morning communion (prayers and affirmations) which consciously set in motion forces that became the keynote of their whole day. They knew the power of holding a positive thought throughout the day. The natural law that two things cannot occupy the same space at the same time was clear to them. They reasoned that if the mind is filled with positive, creative, harmonious thoughts, there would be no room for inharmonious thoughts. They knew that holding a transpersonal attitude in the mind would calm the whole organism. Facts known to the Essenes about how to introduce ideas into the sub-conscious mind have been rediscovered by modern psychology.

The Essenes made great use of the will. They used the will to master their feelings and to maintain their health and healing techniques. They examined motives, feelings, and choices. They used creative imagery to create energy. Practicing their rituals required continued use of the will. They believed that every great value in human culture owes its creation to the exercise of the will to stay in contact with the energies of the Creator.

The Essenes believed that definite irrefutable laws govern the universe—plants, animals, persons, communities—and that these laws are available to those who discipline themselves to listen and follow. They believed that nature's laws cannot be revised. Interfering with the laws would surely result in disharmony, disruption, and negativity.

They called the natural law governing the human mind the Law of Attitudes. Simply stated, the Law is to express unconditional love towards the self, others, and the Source of life—with the whole mind in all action and thought. The Eight Attitudes are expressions of this Law, and together they represent the *Code of Conduct*.

Unconditional Love and Forgiveness is a study of this Code. From this study we will find great wisdom concentrated in a few rules. Part One examines the basic concepts: *Naphsha,* attitudes, goals, and the will. Part Two presents the Law of

Attitudes and the Eight Attitudes. Part Three offers the heart of my work: the essential teachings and techniques for practicing unconditional love and forgiveness, which I have found to be successful throughout many years of practice. The unique process of forgiveness (chapters 15 and 16) has proved at workshops throughout the world to be immensely beneficial for those desiring to free themselves of hostility and resentment.

Although the Attitudes have been rendered into English, I have left some words in the original Aramaic when no appropriate English word could be found. These basic words represent concepts of love, neighbor, sin, failure, spirit, forgiveness, attitude, law, and the Higher Self. The Aramaic words (defined in the Glossary at the end of the book) convey so much more than our normal connotations of these words. They are simple, more precise, rich in imagery, and they uniquely capture and express the subtleties of transpersonal psychology. For instance, the Aramaic language does not distinguish between mental and physical. It does not divide a person into mental, physical, and emotional parts; it perceives the person as a whole. Nor does Aramaic distinguish between cause and effect; the same word signifies both.

Each of the Eight Attitudes begins: "A transpersonal attitude is theirs . . . ." Transpersonal means exalted above the personality, a higher order, a perfect state or condition above the personal, everyday experience. Transpersonal could also be called an alpha state, one of relaxed, calm objectivity.

The practice of the Law of Attitudes is one of the best insurance policies against building up expectations and demands that detract from our growth and cause us to be disappointed and resentful. As you read and study this Law, remember its ancient origin and how it has been followed by successful people for thousands of years.

Wherever these concepts are taught—with prisoners, alcoholics, drug addicts, as well as with those suffering life-threatening diseases— immediate behavioral and physical changes have occurred. I believe, as do certain others who have researched the Essene *Code of Conduct,* that many global problems are related to a lack of under- standing and application of what the Code sets forth. These concepts can change medical, social, and educational practices and restore wholeness to the world. This book provides step-by-step directions for changing your life into one of productivity and unconditional love for yourself and all humanity. These laws and principles are scientific—they will work every time if you direct your will to achieve relief, health, and peace of mind. You will become the loving, forgiving person you were created to be.

Chapter 2
NAPHSHA
Our Connection with the Source

Naphsha (pronounced *NOFFsha*) is the most important element of this book. Naphsha is our connection with the Source of life, with that higher intelligence that directs the orderly flow of all life. Naphsha is our connection with God.

The Essenes used the word *Naphsha* in several ways. In a number of places in Aramaic literature, the word *Naphsha* has been used as "life," "breath of life," or "breath of God." The following passage appears in some Bibles published in the early 1800s: "And the Lord God formed man of the dust of the ground and breathed into his nostrils Naphsha, and man became a living soul." In later versions this passage is translated: "The Lord God breathed into man's nostrils the breath of life and he became a living soul." (Genesis 2:7).

Some texts translate Naphsha as "Soul," others as "Self" with a capital *S*. Psychosynthesis and other psychological texts also distinguish between the *Self* or *Higher Self,* and the *self* with a lower case *s.* The self (lower case) is referred to as the personal self, the ego, or the *I* with which we identify when we say, "I had a good day." The personal self is the conscious, aware self that makes decisions and choices.

Discussing what might seem to be a duality of the selves, Assagioli states:

There are not really two selves, two independent and separate entities. The Self is one; it manifests in different degrees of awareness and self-realization. The reflection (self) appears to be self-existent, but has, in reality, no autonomous substantiality. It is, in other words, not a new and different light but a projection of its luminous source, the Self.[1]

The drawing on the right shows Naphsha above the personal self. The broken line connecting them, representing fluctuation or change, indicates that there are times when we feel closely connected to Naphsha and times when we may not. Although Naphsha is always available to us, we may not be aware of its presence because we are so active in our personal lives, or because we shut off the connection through our attitudes and actions.

The Self, or Naphsha, and its reflection, the self, have different functions. Some scientists refer to an organism's "controlling core" or "universal unconscious" which directs and coordinates physical, emotional, and mental development and activity. These ideas coincide with those of the Essenes, who believed that Naphsha holds each person's unique design or "blueprint."

Naphsha is whole and cannot be divided without perilous consequence. The Aramaic text, found in the *Khaboris Manuscript,* presents this idea: "Every kingdom which you divide against its Naphsha will decay and every house and city which shall be divided against its Naphsha . . . will not last."[2] This statement indicates that Naphsha controls not only the life force of individuals, but of cities, houses, and kingdoms as well.

The Essenes emphasized that Naphsha is a link between the personal self and the Source (God). Naphsha acts like a transformer, modulating the voltage from the Source so it can be utilized by individuals according to their capacity to handle this energy. This makes Naphsha available to each one of us according to our ability to utilize it.

Naphsha is in contact with all universal laws and communicates these laws to the personal self. The messages will register if the personal self is open and receptive.

Naphsha is the source of healing and wholeness for our physical, emotional, mental, and spiritual aspects. It is a center of vital, life-giving energy. This energy surrounds the physical body and is what scientists refer to as an energy field. An energy field surrounds every living thing—trees, plants, animals, and human beings.

In the body there are what I sometimes call

"energy distribution centers." They are linked with Naphsha and they transform as well as distribute energy. I was once part of a research group of one hundred people. We were put in a large empty room and asked to walk about at random without looking at the other people. There was a lot of bumping into one another. Then we were asked to center ourselves in Naphsha, close our eyes, and walk about in the same manner. This time we did not bump others. We could feel the energy fields of the others and knew when we were getting close to them. I kept seeing a stream of blue light. My inner feeling was to turn away when I saw the blue light, but I decided to continue in the same direction. Each time I did this, I bumped into someone. Not only was I feeling their energy field, I was getting visual warnings as well.

A person's energy field is identical in shape to the physical body and extends a few inches beyond the body's outer dimensions. This energy field, or "etheric body," as some have called it, reflects our state of mind, body, emotions, and attitudes. I have had persons come for counseling who were experiencing feelings of depression. Their eyes were dull, their skin was sallow. They were lifeless. After the counseling session, their eyes were bright, their skin was glowing, and they were alive and energetic. This was brought about by changing the attitude—starting the flow of energy in the etheric body and thereby changing the physical body.

Improper Use of the Will
Impairs Naphsha

Each one of us has a Naphsha or, more precise-
ly, is a Naphsha, by virtue of our existence. We
have a free will. We can go against the Naphsha
or against the laws of nature, including the laws
of health or human relations. Going against
Naphsha is an improper use of the will and can
cause inferior physical, emotional, mental, and
spiritual performance. When we act counter to
Naphsha, through ignorance or through conscious choice, we will experience conflict.
Naphsha sends messages of conflict to our
conscious mind in promptings, feelings of
anxiety, stress, uneasiness, warning dreams,
discontent, and unrest.

The messages and promptings can be shut off,
just as disturbing dreams can be shut off. To
ignore messages from Naphsha requires a strong
and deliberate use of the will. Needless to say,
such avoidance is an improper use of will.

It takes time and great effort to shut down
this powerful, universal communication system.
I feel that one of the reasons many people use
alcohol and drugs is to shut off messages from
Naphsha. Those who ignore these messages also
shut themselves off from intuition, premoni-
tions, and other instinctual experiences.

When Naphsha's messages are shut off from
consciousness, they continue to register unconsciously. It is as though the door bell to the
conscious mind has been disconnected—the

conscious mind does not know the messenger was there or what message was left.

Conflict between the personal self and the Higher Self (Naphsha) is apparent in symptoms of unrest, high blood pressure, various gastro-intestinal ailments, lack of energy, and depression. Perhaps for this reason the ancients referred to Naphsha as the source of healing. Everyone has experienced the "miracle" of having a cut heal a few days after injury. We can conclude that our natural state is one of wholeness. A stream of healing energy flows through us and surrounds us to keep us whole. The origin of that energy is the Source of life, which is directed through Naphsha. This natural healing process is sometimes referred to as the "doctor within" or the "inner healer."

The goal of the healthy individual is to learn how to cooperate with Naphsha and heed its messages. If we have any of the above-mentioned ailments, we need to ask Naphsha what message it has for us.

When we are in contact with Naphsha we take responsibility for our actions. We are willing and able to play a responsible role in our family, community, nation, and the world. When we can contact Naphsha at will we are better able to make wise choices. We can take action with confidence because we see from a place of wisdom. Serenity distinguishes us. Although we may be going through difficult life circum-stances, we remain calm at the center of our being. This inner calm, devoid of emotional disturbance, sustains us. When we are recovering from the death of a loved one, for instance, Naphsha often brings an inner peace beyond ordinary understanding.

Naphsha also brings us a sense of gratitude. I was a guest leader in a farm community which had, earlier that week, been ravaged by a great flood. At dinner I was sitting beside a lady whose home and belongings had been swept down the river. "All my children were saved!" she exclaimed. "My husband and I are well and strong. Oh, we have so much! I feel so grateful for life!" These were the words of a woman, dressed in clothes from the Red Cross, whose house, barn, farm machinery, and livestock were gone forever. Her face was radiant, and there was an energy about her that was joyous and heartwarming. The loss of material things helped her see life in perspective. There was no doubt in my mind that this woman was in touch with her Naphsha.

The very nature of Naphsha is love and goodwill. This is a love beyond love of family and friends. It is a universal, unconditional love. This kind of love can flow through us, heal us, and make us whole. Joy comes into the personality like a flood of energy when we are in harmony with Naphsha.

Group Naphsha

Naphsha is more easily contacted in the presence of a supportive group when group solidarity is present. This produces a feeling of oneness with all beings. The Essenes refer to "group Naphsha," a state in which whole groups of people were able to express transpersonal energy, or the attitude of unconditional love.

I have for years created an atmosphere of group Naphsha in my classes and workshops because participants seem to learn faster and it is more joyous for all. I start this process through my own attitude. Assuming a transpersonal attitude, I view the participants as Naphshas or Higher Selves present in their physical bodies. I assume they are there to learn, to develop their potential. I ask my own Naphsha to give me ideas and insights on how to meet their needs. I do this days in advance as well as immediately prior to and during the event.

In the beginning of a class or workshop, I point out the need to be open and expectant. I ask the participants to visualize a symbol of openness such as an open flower, window, door, or whatever symbol spontaneously comes to mind. Then I ask them to imagine their minds like that open symbol. I ask them to imagine their hearts being open like a flower—a lotus or a rose—opening to the rays of the sun and sending out its fragrance. I ask them to send love out to the members of the group and to accept themselves and others just as they are. This method has proved effective in a number of ways. Let me give an example:

I was to lead a meditation for the Meditation Research Group, of which I was once the director. I was aware of the unity of this group which had been meeting together for months. The love and goodwill had a definite presence in the room that morning. We customarily started each meditation with a silent period. As I became still, I felt prickles, like small needles piercing the skin on the left side of my forehead, accompanied by some pain that seemed to come from an outside source. I had never experienced this.

"What is this?" I asked myself.

"Some in the group need healing," were the words that came into my mind.

"I am not a healer," I said to myself, resisting my inner voice.

"Do you refuse to be used to help others?" I heard inside my head. I knew these messages were not me, the self, but were of a higher dimension and were related to the group. I was unsure of what to say or do, but I felt a willing-ness to be a channel for this power. As the silent period came to an end I felt a great calm come over me.

"Some in the group need healing," I an-nounced in a matter-of-fact way, as though this were a regular occurrence. Everyone was still and attentive. I asked each person to send love and goodwill to everyone present. There was deep silence and stillness. I still did not know what I was going to do.

"In the name of God, the Father, Naphsha, and the Holy Spirit, be healed!" I said aloud, with authority and strength, surprising myself!

The group remained silent, and I continued with the rest of the meditation as usual.

Later, privately and independently, three members who had been seated to my left in the circle reported to me their healing experiences. Was I feeling their pain coming into the left side of my forehead?

One woman said she had pain in her lower back when she came to the group. "I had to make a great effort to get out of the car and come up the steps, the pain was so severe. When you said 'be healed,' the pain quit." This woman had suffered back pain for years. Three years later she told me her back had not hurt since that morning at the Meditation Research Group.

Another person had been involved with a lawsuit for months and was under great stress about what action he should take. "That morning just as you started the meditation I felt great disturbances and pain in my chest. When you said, 'be healed,' it felt like birds flew out of my chest. Then came a great calm and at that instant I knew exactly what to do about my situation. I felt so relieved and have ever since."

The third member was a woman who had noticed six or eight large lumps on her body two days before the group experience. "That night after the meeting, all the lumps were gone," she reported.

I believe the three healings were facilitated by the energy of the group, which had risen to a transpersonal level. We had access to our individual Naphshas and the group Naphsha—the resultant energy flushed out that which was not in harmony with it.

The Naphsha has the job of keeping the body, mind, and emotions balanced and in harmony. Illness is the lack of harmony in some part of us. When the flow of Naphsha's energy in the body is blocked, illness can occur. Naphsha keeps us in harmony with the rest of the universe; it is our connection with the Source of creation.

Chapter 3

ATTITUDES
The Brain's Filters

To understand what the Essene teachings mean for us today, we must understand the concept and function of "attitudes." An attitude is a mind set (a neural structure of the brain) which is a combination of feelings, thoughts, ideas, and memories that color or affect perception. Attitudes serve as filters in the brain. An attitude colors everything that passes through it. Here are two examples of positive and negative attitudes expressed in a living situation:

A manufacturing business has had several recent financial reverses. The controller announces to the executive of this business that a new tax bill has just arrived which is greatly increased over the previous year. The executive has a positive attitude. He replies to the controller, "We will have to find a way to be more productive to cover these extra costs." They proceed to work at the tax problem as well as other matters requiring their attention.

Now let's consider the effects of an opposite attitude in the same situation. When the controller presents the news of the tax increase, the executive goes into a tirade, feels sorry for himself, accuses himself of being a poor executive, and also blames the government. He becomes so filled with negativity that he loses rapport with the controller. He remains upset for a period of time and makes some poor decisions about other unrelated matters.

In another case, a man is ready to leave for work in the morning and discovers his car has a flat tire. He says, "What a good place to have a flat, if I had to have one. My phone is here so I can call for help and I can call work to tell them I may be late. I'm glad it happened here instead of on the freeway."

Someone with an opposite attitude might approach the flat tire saying, "Things like this always happen to me. Those tires are not as good as they should be. I'll bet that salesman sold me a bad tire." This person continues to complain and delays taking care of the problem. The negative attitude does not allow him to see the solution.

Attitude is a term used in navigation. Ray Wilson, a space engineer, states:

> Attitude is a term used in referring to all spacecraft, manned or unmanned satellites, and aircraft. The spacecraft is placed on a course in such an attitude or position for the guidance system to lock on to two reference stars, sun, moon, earth, or some combination. A change resulting from either an internal or external disturbance may cause a wrong attitude. Consequently, it loses its "fix" on the contact stars and proper direction. It may even select other stars which could cause it to miss target. To correct course it is necessary to change the attitude of the craft (such as putting it in a slow roll), let the sensor search for and lock on to the proper star, send out feedback to the control station for verification and course direction, if necessary.

Communication and control of human behavior also depend on attitude. If we adopt the wrong attitude, communication is difficult and course correction is required. How does attitude affect behavior? The human brain and nervous system have remained a deep mystery to most of us because we have assumed that brain functioning was too complex for us to understand. However, research in the last twenty-five years is providing new insights and is helping us to see the brain as a new frontier for dynamic discoveries.

We are learning that, somewhat like the computer, the human brain brings together goals, attitudes, beliefs, wishes, desires, facts, and fantasies into an automatic pattern of functioning which produces certain behaviors. Like the computer, the brain can only work with what it is given. The brain and computer automatically follow a routine process except when that process is interrupted with additional information or ideas. The brain is a most sensitive organ and responds to the slightest suggestion or stress.

The basic functioning unit of the nervous system is the neuron. There are only two kinds of neural activity: activating and inhibiting. Activating neuron energy causes other neurons to fire. This firing tends to produce movement. Inhibiting neuron activity causes other neurons to resist activation. All neural activity falls in one or the other of these two processes. An estimated eighty percent of the brain's more than thirty billion neurons are engaged in the inhibiting process.

The brain receives data through a complex transmission process whereby sensory information is translated into electrical representations and then delivered to the brain along neural pathways by electrical impulse. The more intense a stimulus, the more rapid the firing of the neural chain. Different neural pathways transmit diverse types of stimulations. The brain receives sensory input from three sources: the external environment; the physical body; and mind recall, or memory.

The external environment brings to our perception sounds from traffic, an airplane overhead, music from the room next door, the smell of food cooking, awareness of the colors in the room, and intensity of light from the window. In the body we are aware of our throat being dry, a feeling of embarrassment flushing our face, our eyes feeling moist, uneasiness in the pit of our stomach, and the tenseness of some of our muscles.

Memory is stimulated by experience. As we pick up a piece of chalk we may remember standing at the chalkboard in fifth grade. The teacher is asking us to work out a math problem. We remember getting the right answer and feeling proud. These and other memories are recalled and incorporated into the electrical impulses sending the data to the brain.

As many as ten thousand units of information can come into the brain per unit of time. We would literally "blow our minds" if we could not filter out some of this information. Goals and attitudes serve as filters to screen out the excess stimuli; these stimuli are selected according to the goals and attitudes held at that moment in the mind. Our personal judgments determine which stimuli are processed. All other stimuli are inhibited or screened out of awareness.

For example, it is shortly after noon and I am hungry. I'm driving on a busy street in a strange town, and my goals are to find a restaurant to ease my hunger and to drive safely. My attitude is hopeful, pleasant, eager. My judgment is helping me select the restaurant that appears to have the type of food I can afford, financially as well as nutritionally. I have two "inhibiting" tasks that fit with my goals. Although both sides of the street are lined with storefronts, I notice only those that have food. I notice no makes of cars, I see no license plates. Then I see a supermarket. "There is plenty of safe parking and I can satisfy my hunger with something from the market," flashes into my mind. I recall a quiet park, some fresh fruit, and a sandwich made from grocery store purchases. I also remember that "I'd like a tall glass of iced tea." I am off the supermarket idea and again looking for a restaurant. I see just the place—it reminds me of one in the past that was pleasant and satisfactory. I park and go in.

Perception of what is about us is individual. We block all stimuli that seem irrelevant to our particular desires or goal. We perceive what we wish to perceive and very little else. If the mind does not wish to perceive something, it is not there for that mind. Research with animals and humans in the last several years supports the fact that the inhibitory system shuts off everything except what we choose to attend to.

Recently I visited a big clinic housed in the gymnasium of an old school building. About every three minutes there was a terrible hammering, clanging sound from the exposed water pipes overhead. I asked the receptionist, "Why are they beating on the pipes?" She explained, "Oh, the steam builds up and then releases. That goes on all the time but I don't hear it. I have shut it out of my consciousness."

Maintaining Attitudes through Speech

I recall leading a weekend workshop on a mountain in Southern California. It rained the entire weekend. The road down the mountain was unpaved for half a mile and there were ditches on each side. Before the group departed, I felt led to give some directions for returning safely down the mountain under these conditions. The directions were: "Look where you want to go! If you want to stay in the center of the road, keep your eyes 100% of the time right in the center of the road." Everyone drove safely through the slick mud to the pavement. Since that time, my directions have echoed in my mind as I have created projects and adventures: "Look and see where you want to go!"

We can give direction to the will through words, holding a goal in mind, a visual image, or a combination of a goal, an attitude, and a visual image reinforced by memory. Many books have been written on the subjects of acquiring love, money, happiness, etc., using these methods.

Verbalizing goals and intentions is especially significant. A Russian neuropsychologist by the name of Alexander Luria has noted that humans use speech to harmonize and organize their perceptions, muscular activities, and in many cases, internal bodily functions. He termed the word content of one's brain the "Regulatory Speech System." Normally it is operational at the unconscious level by age six and relatively inflexible by age thirteen.

The purposes or attitudes established through the use of words (even unconsciously) affect behavior and health, or the lack of health. An example of this functioning is the case of a girl who was quite neglected by her parents the first few years of her life. She remembers seeing a classmate in kindergarten getting a great deal of attention because of a broken leg. She longed to have a broken leg or arm so she could receive such attention. She recalls saying over and over, "I wish I could go to the doctor and get a cast on my leg. I wish I could go see the doctor and be loved like Tommy."

Subsequently she had a series of sprained ankles and trips to the doctor. By the time she was sixteen she had spent four months in the

hospital and had undergone several major sur-
geries. She had had thirty-nine blood trans-
fusions because of internal bleeding. After each
surgery she was taken home only to return to the
hospital due to severe illness. Now, at age fifty,
she has had four more major operations. Her
deep, unconscious desire created a willingness to
undergo any amount of pain to get the attention
she so desperately needed.

Silvia Broorstein[1], a psychotherapist, has
used a technique called "Right Speech" with a
number of clients, particularly those whose
speech patterns are hypercritical—who use judgmental terms like "stupid," "good," "bad;" or
who use confrontive language, "tough talk," or
harsh, vulgar, or crude speech.

Right Speech is usually presented and practiced within the context of the Buddhist Eight-
fold Path. Walpola Rahula provides the following explanation in *What the Buddha Taught*:

> Right Speech means abstention 1)from telling
> lies, 2)from backbiting and slander and talk
> that may bring about hatred, enmity, disunity
> and disharmony among individuals or groups of
> people, 3)from harsh, rude, impolite, malicious
> and abusive language, and 4)from idle, useless
> and foolish babble and gossip. When one ab-
> stains from these forms of wrong and harmful
> speech one naturally has to speak the truth, has
> to use words that are friendly and benevolent,
> pleasant and gentle, meaningful and useful.
> One should not speak carelessly; speech should
> be at the right time and place. If one cannot say

something useful, one should keep "noble silence."[2]

Broorstein pointed out to her clients who were overwhelmed with feelings of excessive anger that to continue to say angry things increased their feelings of anger. For those who used judgmental statements, she suggested they substitute "skilled" for "good," and "unskilled" for "bad." Harsh, loud, vulgar, and crude speech was changed into kindly, soft, accurate, and thoughtful words. These clients changed their attitudes towards themselves. As a result of using Right Speech, their self-esteem increased and their relationships became more productive.

The practice of Right Speech involves the use of the will. The will is activated by the choice to refrain from negativity and judgment in our speech. Great care must be exercised by the will to utilize positive speech and to prevent unsound speech in the memory from perpetuating negative life patterns. Many misunderstandings between people stem from a failure to use the will properly to control speech content. Often negative words and behaviors are stored in the unconscious and emerge when we are under great stress.

As we'll see in the next chapter, we can use the will to modify attitudes and thus to effect changes in our lives. The will can be strengthened—much like strengthening a muscle—through proper use. In his book, *The Act of Will*, Roberto Assagioli gives special directions for exercising and strengthening the will.

Chapter 4
THE POWER OF THE WILL

The human will has been the most neglected area of study in Western psychology. Like any other tool, if misused, it will not function properly. Because most people understand so little about the will, they have not used it in positive, creative ways. This ignorance is reflected in the preponderance of illness (both mental and physical), and violence directed towards other people and the environment. Less than ten years ago, when I was researching the subject, I found only twelve books that included any sizable amount of work on the will. Since that time, I am happy to say, there are a great number of books and articles that have been devoted to the will's function.

Although most of us are not conscious of it, we use the will all the time. The will is behind every physical movement or action. Mostly these movements are automatic and we are not aware that we have made a choice. We are not aware of the motivations for our choices.

People addicted to alcohol, food, or drugs often claim they have no will power. The fact is they have plenty! Their will supports their addiction instead of supporting life-giving habits. Their single-minded devotion to achieving their goal—of having that which fuels the addiction—is overwhelmingly strong. The addict will sacrifice job, family, friends, funds, and future in order to achieve the desired momentary goal. If this were a noble sacrifice, the addict would be

said to have great will power, like Joan of Arc or
Gandhi. The fact that the addict's sacrifice is
ignoble does not mean he or she has less will
power. The difference lies in the choice of goals
and attitudes.

We learned in chapter 3 that attitudes are
mind sets controlling what the mind perceives.
They set the course for subsequent behavior.
Goals are specific objectives or desires selected
within that overall framework or course. Establishing the will in relation to a goal takes time.
Once a goal is set, the will becomes established
as a drive for maintaining that goal. Then automatically, faithfully, and unfailingly our mind
seeks to achieve it. In fact, every goal we have
ever made, whether positive or negative, is still
operating in our lives unless we have cancelled or
replaced it.

It's as though the mind were a mail order
house and we placed an order for ten white bed
sheets per month, paid for them (that is, put
energy behind the order), and never cancelled
the order in the next twenty years. That order
would be filled regardless of our circumstances.
It wouldn't matter whether we had a house filled
to the ceiling with bed sheets, or whether we
wanted striped or floral patterns. The order
would continue to be filled unless specifically
cancelled or replaced with another order.

Some goals have more motivation behind
them than others. The goals with the greatest
motivation are those formed on the physical,
emotional, mental, and spiritual levels. A goal

formed on all four levels has our total self involved, and the fulfillment of the goal is assured success. However, goals formed on all four levels are rare. Most of us function only on the physical, emotional, and mental levels—we don't tap into the full circuit that is available to us.

A goal formed on the physical level (related to comfort and pain) and the emotional level (related to feelings and emotions) is a goal with much motivation. While addictive habits are usually related to goals made on these two levels, they will never be cured or cancelled on these levels. To change or remove long-standing habits, we must involve the mental and spiritual levels as well. Alcoholics Anonymous succeeds in helping people overcome addiction to alcohol because the group's philosophy and therapy includes the mental and spiritual levels.

In my therapy work with cancer victims I have discovered that, previous to the cancer diagnosis (usually three to five years), the patient experienced depression and a wish to die. In my view, this deep wish became unconsciously established as a goal, causing a conflict with the will to live. The therapy, based on psychosynthesis, gives the cancer patient an opportunity to cancel the will to die and to make a goal using the will to live. Establishing a purpose for living is crucial to maintaining the will to live.

Actually, many goals are at the subconscious level, including those that have slipped from conscious awareness over time. Thus we may no longer be aware of a destructive goal which is causing seemingly unwanted results, such as illness, failure, addictions, or compulsions. To will activity, thought, or behavior in opposition to a *subconscious* goal accomplishes nothing. The human mind cannot control itself by *direct* application of will. This is why people who can't stay away from the refrigerator when they want to lose weight become so frustrated with their "lack of will power." They are making a superficial attempt to marshal themselves into compliance against stronger, subconscious goals, attitudes, or beliefs that keep the weight on. The mind is actually controlling itself by the *indirect* means of using the will to maintain attitudes.

The proper function of the will, then, is not to control behavior, but rather to control the mind's attitudes and goals. By so doing, the human mind is able to control itself and its environment indirectly. Long ago, the Essenes learned to use the will to set sound attitudes and goals, producing healthful lives. They developed the habit of self-control through indirect means, knowing that straying from this principle would produce tension.

The mind automatically searches for a way to reestablish harmony. When you learn to control your attitudes and goals by proper use of will, the ability will not escape you, whether you acquire it the hard way or find you have always had it!

Motivation

There is much discussion about motivation and its relation to will. Motivation may be defined as the tension created by an existing goal not yet achieved. The mind always seeks to achieve an established goal or eliminate one by inhibitory blocking. The tension created by an unachieved goal can be satisfied in no other way. The relief of tension is the ceaseless pursuit of the functioning mind. The more powerful the tension, the more relentless the pursuit. The application of that irrefutable principle demands that we consider motivation as the inevitable, inescapable result of an unachieved and existing goal.

WILL: The means by which the human mind controls its attitudes and goals.

ATTITUDE: A mind set, established and maintained by the will, that controls what the mind perceives.

GOAL: An objective or desire established and maintained by attitudes and the will.

MOTIVATION: Tension produced by an existing and unachieved goal.

SUCCESS: Relief from tension, gained by the achievement of a goal.

Goals are to a large extent the result of choice. Some goals, such as obtaining food, water, warmth, or fresh air, are based on internal physical needs. But who has not held his breath too long when attempting a long swim underwater, missed a meal when hungry in order to finish a task, shivered and endured discomfort from the cold to enjoy a winter activity, or forgotten thirst in pursuit of victory? Developing proper use of the will requires understanding these concepts and, most importantly, daily practice.

When two or more goals conflict or contradict each other, the one generating the greatest tension (motivation) will be pursued. The conflicting goal usually is blocked by the inhibitory system to reduce tension and reappears when it once again generates the highest degree of motivation. We may not experience hunger working through lunch hour in order to finish a project, but upon its completion, hunger reappears.

To break an undesirable habit, first select a conflicting goal that is positive and desirable, then generate more motivation to achieve it than the undesirable goal. Note the necessity of creating a *positive* conflicting goal! The ball player can't hit the ball by trying not to miss. He must want to hit the ball.

An overweight girl of fourteen set a goal to weigh 110 pounds and to have a beautiful figure. Her greatest temptations were bread, butter, and cookies. On her dressing table she placed a small statue of a beautiful nude woman. As she looked at the statue she drew in her abdomen muscles and held herself erect, like the statue. She was aware of how proud she felt of her own figure as she imagined it thin and shapely. She cut out magazine pictures of lovely girls in swimsuits and put the pictures on the bread drawer, the refrigerator, and the cookie jar. Within a few months she weighed 110 pounds and had a beautiful figure. That was fifteen years ago—she still is slim and beautiful.

The more often we repeat our goal, using words and images, the greater our motivation to fulfill that goal. Reminders of the goal create greater motivation for fulfilling it.

Motivation is measured by the number of neural conflicts resolved by a goal's achievement. Raising or increasing motivation for the positive conflicting goal will automatically cancel or inhibit the goal which is producing the undesirable habit. This process ends the habit as long as the sound goal has the higher degree of motivation.

These general principles govern the cancelling of an unwanted goal and its replacement with a desired goal:

1. The conflict between goals will always be resolved in favor of the goal generating the higher degree of motivation.

2. The more reasons for attaining the goal, the higher its degree of motivation.

3. The more frequent the reminders, verbal and/or sensory, the higher its degree of motivation.

4. When achievement repeatedly reduces tension, the goal "fixes" and becomes permanent.

Attitudes Affect Goals

There is considerable interaction between attitudes and goals. Attitudes control input to what is processed by the mind. Goals initiate the mind's output, in the forms of judgment, behavior, or action. Every goal necessarily includes an attitude that "tunes" the input filters of the mind. For instance, we may have a goal to do something for someone else. If the goal is injurious to that person, and if we maintain love for that person, we will be unable to carry out the goal of injury. It will be blocked or inhibited as long as our mind maintains love for the person.

If in this case we did not have the attitude of love for our neighbor (in Aramaic, anyone of whom we are aware), Naphsha would create severe tension within the body, mind, and emotions. We might be able to will to shut off such tension and block Naphsha's message from consciousness, but the tension would continue unconsciously with the same force, causing conflict and physical stress. If we reached the goal and caused harm, Naphsha would create even more tension. Such a conflict may eventually result in disease and death.

The Buddha is quoted as saying, "When one person hates another, it is the hater who falls ill—physically, emotionally, and spiritually. When he loves, it is he who becomes whole. Hatred kills, love heals."

When we have deep emotions and feelings, that is the time to "plant" ideas in the unconscious, to communicate to the will to set a goal. However, again, this goal must be positive in every way. It must not harm or limit ourselves or others. Times of emotional upset are the times we most need to practice harmlessness towards ourselves and others.

Pete

Pete was a boy of fifteen. His parents were unhappy with each other and there was much tension in the home. Pete was the eldest son and was close to his mother. He was tall, thin, had severe acne, and thought he was the ugliest human being alive. Although his mother pressured him to go out and make friends, he stayed in the house most of the time. If he was asked to go on an errand, he crossed the street to avoid the neighborhood boys. He hated himself and often said he wished he could die.

At school Pete was shy. He had no friends and his grades were just passable. He continued this pattern of self-hate throughout high school and into college. When the acne cleared up in his third year of college, he began to think about his future. He decided to become a physician. Although his social life remained poor, his grades improved drastically. He entered medical school, studied hard, and performed well.

He specialized in plastic surgery and received encouragement and opportunities in this field from an admiring professor. Just as he finished his residency, he met an attractive colleague and they eventually married. He opened offices in a large city and started his practice. Everything was going well.

A group of doctors in the area near Pete's office met on a regular basis to share their work. Pete enjoyed these meetings and appreciated the opportunity to learn from the others. One day Pete shared some of his own work and was questioned about it by another young doctor. The other doctor disagreed with Pete's treatment of the patient, even though the patient did very well and had an excellent recovery. Pete felt criticized and hurt; he became reluctant to attend subsequent meetings despite his wife's urgings. The more she pressured him, the more he was reminded of his mother who had pressured him to socialize with his peers.

Pete became depressed and withdrew from his wife. His practice suffered; his health began to suffer. Two years from the time he began his practice he discovered he had Hodgkins' disease. Pete gave up his practice and sought special sources of healing.

When he first came to me, Pete had conflicts about his will to live. The part of him that identified with his medical training did not believe he could be well. Much of the conflict related to his estrangement from his wife. As we worked together, Pete discovered it was he who had closed himself off from her. Since he had been so withdrawn, he had not been aware of her love. He began to appreciate her and her caring for him; they renewed their relationship and Pete began to make much progress.

For a period of time, Pete talked of wanting to live. His spirit was lifted, and we began to consider his purpose for living. He did not want to go back to plastic surgery, but talked of specializing in holistic health.

Pete lived 500 miles from me. He was receiving treatment at the university medical school in his city and found it difficult to continue therapy with me. I referred him to a psychotherapist in his city. He phoned me occasionally for the next year or so. Later I visited Pete and he told me that he had decided to die. I felt I wanted to do something for him. I asked him if he would like to finish any "unfinished business." He said yes, he would like to forgive the young doctor who had offended him in the medical meetings and whom he had been hating all this time.

I assisted him in forgiving this man. Pete breathed deep sighs of relief, then allowed love to flow into himself from the Source and out to the young doctor. He looked peaceful as color returned to his face. Pete died about two weeks after my visit.

Depression and a deep wish to die are traceable factors in a high percentage of cancer patients with whom I've worked. I assist such people in reversing the decision to die if they wish. Reversing the decision to die and establishing a will and a purpose for living are strong forces in helping them transform their lives.

A deep wish to die, one which is repeated inwardly with deep emotion, is accepted as a goal by the will. A goal against life always causes a conflict within the individual and will be expressed later as disease. Hate directed towards the self creates discord and conflict within and will eventually cause disease. When we are depressed and suffering great mental agony, we may consciously view death as a way of stopping pain, of providing sweet relief. As time passes, there is a lessening of the depression and apparent recovery from it, as in Pete's case. He returned to normal life, unaware of his goal to die—the deep unconscious wish set by the will to produce results.

As a youth Pete suffered from acne, disliked his appearance, and often stated verbally his wish to die. This was no doubt accepted by the will as a goal. Deep negative feeling accompanied the death wishes. His image of the outside world, in childhood and adulthood, was of danger; he feared being overpowered and being taken advantage of. Even though it took years for Pete's goals to be fulfilled, they were constantly operating unconsciously and eventually were brought to fruition.

Pete's story illustrates the incredible power of the will and the importance of using deeply emotional experiences to plant positive goals or ideas in the unconscious. We should frame no judgments and cease all action and goal formation while our attitudes are negative. Unsound subconscious goals may be activated, as in Pete's case. While attitudes are positive, sound goals (conscious and unconscious) may be achieved.

Rest and meditation provide a period in which the degree of motivation behind each goal may be readjusted by the will and brought into greater conformity with nature's laws. In the Essene Code it is written, "One who wishes to be whole (healthy) must love the Source of life with one's whole being, must love oneself and all others of which one is physically and mentally aware." The Eight Attitudes in the Code are based upon this primary law.

To hold the attitude of love towards the Source, self, and others is setting the tone of our lives. To hold this attitude as a goal for our lives is the basic message of the Code and of this book.

The importance of having sound goals in our lives cannot be overestimated. We need to set positive goals and review them often. The Naphsha is the source of the positive attitudes which are formulated and kept in place by the will. Proper use of the will means setting attitudes and goals at the spiritual level--by connecting with our Naphsha.

Exercise for the Proper Use of the Will

This exercise involves some writing. Goal Sheets for this purpose appear on pages 54 and 55. Before filling in the sheet you may wish to photocopy them in order to have blank sheets for additional goals.

1. Select a simple, positive goal and write it in the space provided on the Goal Sheet. (E.g., "I will to comfortably stand still for ten minutes," or "I will to comfortably be silent for twenty minutes.") Then select a goal related to some daily routine, like dressing in the morning.

2. In the space provided, write five advantages of achieving the selected goal and five disadvantages which will result from not achieving the goal.

3. Review your goal three times daily. Visualize the goal being accomplished.

4. On the back of the Goal Sheet, write results obtained each day. At bed time, review the written reports from previous days.

5. Upon achieving your goal comfortably—and comfort should be a part of each goal—select a new positive goal. This time, select a goal whose achievement will break some slight unwanted habit. Repeat steps 2, 3, and 4 with this second goal until it also is comfortably achieved.

6. Upon achieving this second intermediate goal, select a positive goal whose achievement conflicts with a persistent, deep-rooted negative habit. Repeat steps 2, 3, and 4 with this goal until it also is comfortably achieved. Depending on the goal, it may take several weeks or months to accomplish such a goal. Remember, it took time to establish the habit and it takes time to change it.

Upon achievement of the third and most difficult goal, you should possess the power of your will to accomplish whatever you wish! If you do not comfortably make the jump from intermediate to difficult, simply drop back and work on a less trying goal, then step forward again. You are now learning one of the most important lessons in life.

Goal Sheet

State your goal briefly. Always add the word "comfortably" in the goal:

I will to comfortably————————————

————————————————————

Benefits I will experience in achievement of this goal:

1. ————————————————————

2. ————————————————————

3. ————————————————————

4. ————————————————————

5. ————————————————————

Disadvantages from failure to achieve this goal:

1. ————————————————————

2. ————————————————————

3. ————————————————————

4. ————————————————————

5. ————————————————————

Goal Sheet

State your goal briefly. Always add the word "comfortably" in the goal:

I will to comfortably_____

_____

Benefits I will experience in achievement of this goal:

1. _____

2. _____

3. _____

4. _____

5. _____

Disadvantages from failure to achieve this goal:

1. _____

2. _____

3. _____

4. _____

5. _____

Part
Two

THE LAW OF ATTITUDES; THE EIGHT ATTITUDES

The Essene *Code of Conduct* consists of the Law of Attitudes and the Eight Attitudes. The Essenes took the laws for living from ancient revelations from the Source-God. The Code was handed down from generation to generation for thousands of years. As new revelations came from the Source they were added to the Code. The Essenes believed that definite irrefutable laws governed the operation and existence of all things in the universe. They studied these laws constantly and lived by them.

The Law of Attitudes

The Law of Attitudes has three parts:

The First Law is to love the Source of our life, our Creator, with our whole self—in all of our actions and in all of our thoughts. Its purpose is to keep us "tuned in" to the Source of life and to the fact that love is the basis of nature's laws.

The Second Law is to love ourself as a creation of the Source. We are to love our physical body and care for it and keep it well; to love our emotional life, with its great capacity to feel; to love our mental life, with its ability to think, plan, and reason; and to love our Naphsha, that is directly connected to the Source of all creation, the source of our wisdom, compassion, unconditional love, and ability to forgive.

The Third Law is to love unconditionally all those of whom we are physically or mentally aware. They are also creations of the Source and are directly connected to us.

The Eight Attitudes

Each of the Eight Attitudes begins with: "A transpersonal attitude is theirs (touvey-houn). . . ." *Touvey* is an Aramaic noun referring to a part of the brain which has a heavenly dignity and function, desired by the Creator for all human minds. It makes available to each person thoughts and actions which are in harmony with the will of a loving God, for increased happiness and well-being. *Houn* is a plural suffix indicating personal human possession.

The attitudes recommended in this course of study bring into consciousness the transpersonal qualities that enhance and invigorate our daily lives and help make us conscious of the dynamic power which is available to us at all times. This power, this vital life, this spiritual wisdom is ours by an act of our will. All we have to do is live the Eight Attitudes.

The First Attitude

A transpersonal attitude is theirs,
those whose home is in Rukha;
theirs is a transpersonal state.

The Second Attitude

A transpersonal attitude is theirs,
those conscious of their wrongs;
they shall be cured of their mental stress.

The Third Attitude

A transpersonal attitude is theirs,
those with humility;
they will gain the earth.

The Fourth Attitude

A transpersonal attitude is theirs,
those who hunger and thirst for
justice and fairness;
they shall attain it.

The Fifth Attitude

A transpersonal attitude is theirs,
those whose love is without conditions;
they will therefore receive unconditional love.

The Sixth Attitude

A transpersonal attitude is theirs,
those without faults in their minds;
they will see the Source.

The Seventh Attitude

A transpersonal attitude is theirs,
those serving the peace of the Creator;
they will be called the heirs of the Source.

The Eighth Attitude

A transpersonal attitude is theirs,
those being scorned and harrassed
and having evil spoken against them
because of their stand for justice and right
  behavior;
theirs is one of complete inner peace and
  serenity.

Chapter 6
THE FIRST ATTITUDE
The Attitude of Home in Rukha

From the ancient Essene *Code of Conduct* the First Attitude reads thus:

A transpersonal attitude is theirs *(touveyhoun)*
whose home *(masken)* is in *rukha;*
theirs is a transpersonal state *(malkoota
d'shmeya).*

The Aramaic word *masken* means home, lair, den, abode; a place of rest. "Rest" in Aramaic means physical, emotional, and mental rest. Home is thus a place where one rests, recharges, and revitalizes the self; a place of emotional ease and security; a place of mental relaxation and peace of mind.

Rukha is rendered in Aramaic as spirit, essence, energy, force. In psychology it would be a transpersonal energy beyond personal concerns. To have one's home or place of rest in a transpersonal state would be above all concern, a place of seeing the personality (physical, emotional, mental) as the place of trial and error. On this transpersonal level, one is able to see life as it is, as advocated in the Sixth Attitude.

Rukha is also referred to in Aramaic as an invisible force or pressure of nature such as electricity, wind, or magnetism. *Rukha (d'koodsha)* is a force from the Creator that transforms the effects of wrongdoing. It is that portion of the creative force which pressures for soundness in human relationships.

The First Attitude indicates a way of achieving mental and emotional rest. To find such rest, according to the ancient Code, we must achieve that higher-than-usual state of mind. We need to raise our consciousness and find rest in the invisible force of rukha, the force which is able to break up or change the effects of wrongdoing. Could this be "the peace of mind which is beyond ordinary understanding?" If we could comprehend all things, see one's motives and intentions, we no doubt would understand our fellow beings. The Sixth Attitude tells us that only when our minds are clear and pure can we see things as they truly are. Someone once said, "If we could read the secret history of our enemies, we would find in each man's life sorrow and suffering enough to disarm all hostility."

The Essenes recommended assuming the attitude of home in rukha at the beginning of each day, thus setting the tone for the day's experiences. If we start the day on a transpersonal level, aware of the spiritual energies available to us, this attitude will color or influence our perceptions. We will be able to see things in a fresh light, above the illusions of everyday consciousness and public opinion.

A manufacturing company's management asked its foremen to begin each day by listing all the tasks to be done that day. The company became much more productive than it had been. Management next asked the foremen not only to list jobs to be done that day, but to visualize the jobs being done with ease and employee cooperation. Again the company was astounded to see that production levels far exceeded projections and also that company morale greatly improved. This experiment demonstrates the attitude of home in rukha— seeing how the situation could be at its best and effectively creating a positive group attitude.

The Essenes were aware of how the resting mind operates. Before retiring in the evening they followed the disciplines of cleansing or emptying the mind of disharmony and of opening the consciousness to home in rukha. Is it any wonder that they were more productive personally and agriculturally than their neighbors who were constantly at war?

Holding the attitude of home in rukha, as well as the other attitudes of the Code, creates an atmosphere about you and those with whom you associate that others can sense. This transpersonal state is called *malkoota d'shmeya*. It is described as clean, sound, wholesome, happy, desirable. Malkoota d'shmeya means "the way it ought to be," a more perfect condition with the companion benefits of happiness, health, efficiency, and relaxed pleasure.

Home in rukha is an attitude we are invited to assume. It is a mind set—a filter for the mind (as all attitudes are). If, each day, we were to assume the transpersonal attitude of being at home in rukha, we could raise our consciousness above emotions, such as impatience with ourselves and others for not meeting expectations and demands. In our place of physical, emotional, and mental rest we could be free of stress, and experience health and wholeness. Nothing would disturb our peace of mind.

A Morning Exercise in Home in Rukha

On waking in the morning, stand and stretch slowly and gently. Breathe deeply and slowly, six deep breaths. Now sit with your back straight, and close your eyes. Be aware of your body—let it be relaxed. Reach up in consciousness (raising your awareness above your head). Imagine home in rukha as a center of light and rest above your head.

Feel gratitude for the rest and sleep of the night and for the new day!

Become aware of your ability to set goals by using your will. Now make a statement of will, such as, "I will to hold comfortably this attitude of home in rukha all this day. I will to have a spirit of calm gentleness about me all this day."

Be aware of your body and your breathing. Breathe deeply, open your eyes, and go forth in peace.

An Evening Exercise in Home in Rukha

Before starting this exercise, I suggest you make a will statement: "I will to stay awake, aware, and alert during this exercise."

Select a quiet place. Sit in a comfortable chair or on the floor in a relaxed position. Relax the body by breathing deeply and quietly, completely filling and slowly emptying the lungs. Be conscious and aware that life is breathing you. (You can alter your breath, but you cannot stop breathing.) *Pause.*

Feel deep gratitude that life is flowing through you and causing your heart to beat. Feel yourself a part of that great life force, and feel gratitude for it. *Pause.*

Feel love for the Source of life for designing such a beautiful life for you. *Pause.*

Now imagine your Naphsha as a great light, like the sun above your head. Pause. Imagine a beam of light flowing down into your mind and body. *Pause.* In your consciousness move up that beam of light, above the Naphsha, into the home in rukha, that center of a feeling of calm energy. *Pause.* Experience a deep peace and rest. *Pause.* Let that spirit which is sound, wholesome, happy, and desirable fill your consciousness. *Pause.* Let it fill your mind and rest there—be at home in that spirit of rest and peace. *Pause.*

Be at rest, allowing this spirit of peace to fill you, healing you and restoring you to perfect balance. *Pause.* See and feel your body healed and healthy, strong and vital. Let yourself rest in your home in rukha. *Pause.* Allow this energy of rukha which surrounds you to cleanse and heal all your emotions and feelings—just accept this. *Pause.*

Allow this mental rest and peace to fill your mind and heal it of all concerns. Rest here awhile (stay conscious). Feel the rest and peace. *Pause.*

Now feel the energy, the essence of rukha flowing through your whole being, giving you peace and security. *Pause.*

Be aware of the energy, the feeling of rest and well-being. Allow yourself to stay here for a few moments, feeling deep gratitude for the rest. *Pause.*

Be willing now to let this force of rukha flow through you and out to all your relationships. *Pause.* Direct this feeling of well-being to your family, friends, and fellow beings. Radiate out, as beams of light, this feeling of wholeness. *Pause.* By an act of will, send out this spirit of home in rukha and release any strain in any of your relationships. See all your relationships as positive. *Pause.* Imagine all tensions being dissolved. See everyone as joyous. *Pause.* Now send out beams of light to all humanity. *Pause.*

Now be aware of the beam of light flowing down to your own personality, the mental, emotional, and physical body. *Pause.* Now move down that beam of light and become aware of your physical body. *Pause.* Become aware of your breathing. Become aware of the room where you are and how you are sitting. Now open your eyes and look at your surroundings.

You are now ready to continue with your activities, at the same time holding a subjective attitude which will bring back the feelings of rest and well-being.

You may, if you wish, tape this exercise and listen to it as often as you wish. (Should you become over-stimulated by using the tape or doing the exercise, discontinue it for a day or so.) I highly recommend this exercise if you feel upset, burdened by concerns, or if you just need to rest.

Chapter 7

THE SECOND ATTITUDE
The Attitude that Cures Mental Stress

The Second Attitude reads thus:

A transpersonal attitude is theirs,
those conscious of their wrongs *(abilii)*;
they shall be cured of their mental stress
   (nitbeyoun).

The word *abilii* refers to a sect of Hebrews devoted to social truth, who readily and frequently professed and bewailed their own wrongs and the wrongs of their society. No doubt abilii is used to indicate the need to profess our errors rather than hide or hold on to them. The word *nitbeyoun* actually means "shall be cured of mental stress." There is no one word or symbol in English to convey the idea of freedom from mental stress.

In our culture, becoming conscious of our wrongs brings no comfort—we agonize over them. Because awareness of our errors is so painful, we deny their existence. We strive for outer perfection and are much more interested in appearances than we are in seeing or correcting our mistakes.

In the Aramaic language a wrong simply means not right, or "missing the mark." I read recently of an incident that occurred in a country whose culture is quite different from ours. A man was called before the community council because he had taken some grain from his neighbor's field. When he was on the stand he said the neighbor's fence had a hole in it where he went through to get the grain. The council decided the man whose fence was not in good repair was also missing the mark. They then decided that both the man who owned the fence and the man who took the grain should repair the fence. That was the end of the case. There are many ways of viewing things. Perhaps we ought to be more concerned about how we are contributing to the delinquency of others.

According to this Second Attitude, seeing our wrongs helps us find relief. Seeing them allows us to correct them, thereby avoiding missing the mark again. We can reward ourselves for seeing our wrongs. The attitude suggests that we should rejoice when we become aware of our faults. If we truly desire to see our errors, we can set a goal to do so. This is a good opportunity to utilize a will statement, such as, "I will to be aware of my errors."

After we become aware of our errors we can see what to do to correct them. If we cause a car accident, for example, it would be profitable to go through the accident again in our mind and correct the error. We can also correct errors in human relationships by creating the mental images of the actions we wish to implant for the next occasion. An image in the mind can become an action of the will. The action of the will carries the image to completion. If we wish to take a very important action we need to repeat the imaging exercise several times. The more we create the image, the more the will becomes involved in carrying it to fruition.

To show how effective imaging can be, let us review a research project involving three groups of basketball players. Group I practiced throwing the ball at the basket twenty minutes every day for twenty days and was scored on the first and last days. Group II engaged in no practice for twenty days and was scored on the first and last days. Group III spent twenty minutes a day imagining they were throwing the ball into the basket. When they missed, they mentally corrected their aim accordingly. They also were scored on the first and last days. At the end of twenty days, Group I, which practiced daily, improved in score by twenty-four percent. Group II, which did no practice of any kind, showed no improvement. Group III, which practiced only in their imagination, improved twenty-three percent. [1]

What errors in human relations do you need to be aware of? What errors are you making in your character development? What errors are you making in regard to your health habits? What are your beliefs about yourself? Do you regard yourself as one who can change your actions, attitudes, and beliefs? Do you see yourself as one who desires change? Do you have habits that no longer serve you? Where in life are you missing the mark?

We can learn from our errors if we assume the proper attitude of accepting ourselves just as we are—we commit errors, learn from them, and improve our behavior as a result.

The following exercise may help to reduce your personal stress:

An Exercise in
Alleviating Mental Stress

At the end of the day, or any time after five o'clock, find a quiet place. Sit in a comfortable position. Breathe deeply to relax the body. Close the eyes to turn inward. Review your entire day, beginning with what happened thirty minutes ago, then thirty minutes before that, etc. Look at the day's events as though you are looking at a movie. Observe yourself in an objective way, avoiding criticism of yourself or another. Just observe with a detached, objective attitude. You will see things you may regret, but do not allow the regret to come into your feelings during the review. When you have gone backwards through the day to the moment of waking, you have finished the observation part.

Now look at any part of your day you wish had been different. With no criticism, decide now how you could make it different the next time. With that change in mind, imagine yourself in the same circumstances. Now you have a chance to act differently. In your imagination, do so. You may wish to go through it several times to be sure the desired pattern is established. For instance, you may see yourself being impatient with a friend. As you review the incident in your imagination, see yourself as calm. You are aware of an inner calm, and your friend's attitude does not affect you. Doing this every day will help you become aware of missing the mark. Spend no time in regret. Spend your energy changing the scene before it becomes fixed in the brain.

You may wish to check yourself by asking questions such as:

1. Did I maintain a loving attitude today?
2. Did I look for good in others and in circumstances today?
3. Early in the morning, did I set the attitude of being at home in rukha—a place of rest and peace?
4. Was I critical of myself or others today?
5. Did I feel compassion for self and others today?
6. Was I unconditionally loving and forgiving today?

Chapter 8
THE THIRD ATTITUDE
The Attitude of Humility

The Third Attitude reads thus:

A transpersonal attitude is theirs,
those with humility *(makikh);*
they will gain *(nartoun)* the earth.

The Aramaic word *makikh* means humble, respectful, cooperative, peaceful, non-arrogant. The concept is a mental quality of perceiving and cooperating with the positive desires of another.

Humility, like other attitudes, acts as a filter to the mind and controls perception. Humility enables us to see situations, ourselves, and others in proper perspective—to see how they fit into the larger scheme of life. The transpersonal attitude of humility opens our mind to perceive accurately the needs of others as they see them and to desire to meet those needs when it is practical to do so. Without humility the needs of others, as they see them, are blocked from our mind. If we have preconceived notions of what a friend, family member, or co-worker needs, our mind will tend to remove from awareness the existence of any other need. We then turn scanty evidence into "proof" that we have correctly determined the other's needs. Great care must be exercised to maintain humility at all times, so we do not deceive ourselves into thinking we have humility when we do not.

Pierre

"Americans, Americans!" cried Pierre as he came from the restaurant kitchen.

His words sounded like music to the five of us, unable to speak French. It was evening and we'd driven around in circles for over an hour, without being able to find our hotel where other friends awaited our arrival.

Pierre rushed out to us, telling us in broken English that he knew where our hotel was. He had overheard us asking in the restaurant how to get to our hotel and, realizing no one else understood us, offered his help. He first tried to show us on our map, but we couldn't understand which were one-way and which were two-way streets. He then offered to drive our car to the hotel for us. Since we were already anxious, this didn't seem like a good idea.

Suddenly he said, "I go show. Go to your car."

We went to our car and he came from behind the restaurant on his bicycle, waving us into our car. Speaking rapid French, he told us to follow him as he led us through narrow, one-way streets on his bicycle. We followed his white clothes easily through the darkened streets as he guided us right to the door of our hotel.

Our friends greeted us with relief, and we turned to give our gift of money and gratitude to Pierre. He had gone, and no one saw him leave. Since that time we have called this little man our "angel of mercy."

This is a perfect picture of humility. Pierre saw and felt our need and was able and willing to meet it. He performed a great and needed service for us. He performed an act of humility. If he had received our gifts, or if he had charged us for his services, he would still be exercising humility. Humility has to do with the attitude of being able to see the needs of others and having a desire to fulfill them.

The Humble Person is a Good Communicator

One who practices humility develops the ability to listen; to hear the needs of others. Sometimes those needs are only expressed in the tone of voice or in body language. The one who is humble also sees value in others. The humble person is a good communicator. That person not only senses the sometimes unexpressed need of another, but also relates to the one in need in a sensitive, appropriate manner. At times this requires a great measure of finesse, as well as patience. Although he may already have seen another's need, he can ask about the sensed need and allow the other to express it in his own way and with his own sense of timing.

Nartoun is a verb meaning to gain or earn. This Aramaic word represents an earned gain, not an inherited gain. The person with the transpersonal attitude of humility "shall gain the earth." In this sense earth means as great as the earth—in other words, all-inclusive, expansive, whole, complete, broad. It is saying that the person with the attitude of humility will gain all that is needed, all he or she can use. This is the only transpersonal attitude in the Essene *Code of Conduct* that refers to material gain. The other attitudes have to do with spiritual gain or with the qualities of life.

Let us go back to meeting the needs of others. A need is not a want, a desire, or a wish. A need is a necessity! Needs are basic and essential to our life and well-being. When you learn correctly what is needed by another, be sure to determine whether it is practical for you to meet that need. If you can serve that person by meeting the need, you both will prosper.

We were having a weekend workshop where people were coming from out of town. Knowing they would need a lodging reference, I checked with a motel. When the clerk quoted the price of the rooms, I told her I would be interested in lower-priced rooms. She then told me of a nice motel three blocks away for ten dollars less. I had such a warm feeling towards this lady and her motel chain. She felt my need and met it. A year later my husband and I were traveling in another state and needed a motel. We had a choice of three, one of which belonged to the chain that had referred me to the lower-priced motel. There was no question which motel we chose. The humble clerk who had supplied my need generated repeat business and ultimately made money for her company. This is what we mean by gaining the earth.

People who specialize in recognizing and meeting the needs of others, and who understand the difference between needs and wants, will always be employed. Their goods and services will be in demand. During the Great Depression those with humility were able to provide for themselves. They may have become unemployed because of business closures and various other reasons, but they began to look at the needs of others and started supplying those needs; they started "earning the earth."

When I work with people who are unemployed, I have them list all the things they are skilled at and enjoy. I urge them to find a place such as the Red Cross, hospitals, rest homes, churches, or schools where they can give these services—without pay, if necessary. When they are willing to do this and really want to work, a job always opens up. Sometimes two or three jobs become available through applications my clients have made earlier, but these openings usually arise only after the person has been willing to meet the needs of others.

A former minister had been terminated from his personnel position in a large business firm. He could not find a job anywhere. Pointing out the great service he would be rendering, I suggested he get a job washing dishes in a restaurant. He felt he was too good for that. I then suggested he find a better one, and he got a job loading baggage on a ship. After working for several months he came in and said, "I'm tired of loading suitcases. I think I have more to offer than this." I agreed with him. Then he got a job as an insurance adjuster. In about three months he came in and said, "I think this job is not right for me." I agreed. Then I asked, "What would you really like to do that would serve the needs of people?" He became Activities Director of Senior Citizens of Los Angeles County, a very responsible position. He did an excellent job and provided a great service to those older people. He stayed with that job until he retired years later.

This man was not a humble person when he came to me. He had to learn humility through his experiences. Not until he shifted his center of interest from self to meeting the needs of others did he begin to "earn the earth" and really enjoy his work.

Humility, a Step Towards Intuition

When we practice the attitude of humility our intuition becomes available to us. Humility elevates us above our own personality concerns to a transpersonal level where intuitive ideas are available and abundant. When they first come to us, intuitive ideas do not seem strange or "off-the-wall" but just good sense. Later, when are back at the personality level, we are sometimes astounded at their wisdom. For this reason it is wise to record the ideas immediately—write them down, tape them, or illustrate them in some way.

When I am to see a new client in counseling, I

prepare for the first appointment by becoming aware of my deep desire to meet this person's needs. I raise my consciousness into the trans-personal level and ask if there is anything I need to know about this person. I usually see the person's outline like an x-ray. I sometimes see physical dis-ease (that is, perhaps not specific disease, but a person who is not at ease) and I gain insight as to the cause. Sometimes I see symbols of their relationships which give me clues. I just hold these ideas in my mind. Such information provides the guidance I need for the interview.

One afternoon a thirty-eight-year-old woman came to me, saying that her doctor wanted her to have marriage counseling. Her husband com-plained that she was a hypochondriac because she had gone to a number of doctors who could find no cause for her headache.

I could see she was suffering. I felt compassion for her. Within me was a deep desire to meet her real need. As she described her headache, I saw in my imagination a tumor the size of a small grapefruit. I felt a sense of urgency. I said, "You must go to a neurologist at once!" She said, "I know of none," so I pulled out the telephone directory. The names of three neurologists stood out on the page like neon signs. I copied them down and handed them to her. "You must go now—this afternoon," I told her. She seemed agreeable.

She offered to pay me. I said, "No, use that money for the neurologist. Let me hear from you. I want to know how you get along."

Six weeks later I received a letter from this woman stating that the neurologist put her in the hospital that same afternoon and operated on her later that night.

"He removed a tumor from my brain that was the size of a small grapefruit [her description]. I'm fine, with the exception of having a slight paralysis in my right leg. The doctor thinks I will overcome this in time. He told me if I had waited any longer, I could have had a permanent paralysis of my whole lower spine and legs."

Those who seek to profit by meeting the needs of others may fail, however, unless they first consult others about their needs. For example, a California building contractor went to Amarillo, Texas, where the land is as flat as a table, and purchased a tract of land. He built California-style houses with big picture windows. The houses were built close to one another so the contractor could fit many houses onto the land, and the big picture windows faced those of the other nearby houses. The people of Amarillo were not interested in that type of house. They valued houses with privacy, with windows to let in light and air but little else. The California builder could not sell his houses at any price, and the project sat for years without a single buyer. Had he first determined accurately the needs of his potential buyers, he would have found greater success.

Another transpersonal quality that is a great help in establishing the attitude of humility is silence. We need to do more than just listen. We need to allow the deep inner silence of the trans-personal state to pervade our consciousness and "wash away" our busy-ness and activity so we can hear the wisdom as it comes to us from the transpersonal level. "Silence is the language of God; it is also the language of the heart," Dag Hammarskjold said. "The more faithfully you listen to the voice within you, the better you will hear what is sounding outside. And only he that listens can speak. . . ."[1]

We might say that silence + wisdom + service = humility. The humble person who serves others is in frequent contact with the Higher Self (Naphsha). Humility enables us truly to serve the needs of others.

Practicing Humility

Now that you clearly understand the attitude of humility you are invited to make a decision to practice humility for a certain length of time—a day, half a day, a week, or however long you desire. As you go about your daily life, listen for the needs of others. Notice how they express their needs. Some clearly say, for example, "I need a certain amount of money to meet my needs."

There is a story of a group of people who were praying to God for money. The archangels in heaven were questioning each other, "What is money?" Then, they listened again. The words came back, "Oh, God, give us money, send us money, we need money." The archangels conferred again. They said, "They are really in earnest, but we don't have money or even know what it is. Let's send them some ideas. Maybe they can use them to make money."

Ask yourself, "Is this really her need?" If you supplied the actual amount she states she needs, would her needs be met? For how long? Or does she really need a creative idea which will help her supply her financial needs for years to come? You may need to call upon a wisdom higher than that of your personal self. A transpersonal level of consciousness is available to you. By asking, "How can I truly meet her need?" at that higher level of all-knowing, you may come up with an idea.

Be willing to take the answer as it comes to you. If it seems impractical for you to meet her need at the moment, you may see at a later time how you can serve her, perhaps by referring her to another or giving her a book or a suggestion. Look and listen throughout the time you have designated to practice humility, then meet the needs when it is practical for you to do so.

As your scope widens, you may wish to practice humility all the time. When you see needy people on television or hear them on the radio, ask yourself, "What do they really need?" If you can supply that need, do so. If they need love and understanding, put forth effort to understand them and send your heartfelt love out to them at that moment. As you learn to practice humility you will be greatly rewarded in the service you can render spiritually as well as physically. Often, one who is truly served is willing to show gratitude in material ways.

Meditation on Humility

Humility is a transpersonal attitude. Meditation helps us reach transpersonal realms.

Sit quietly, either in a chair or on the floor. You should be comfortable but never prone when meditating. Sit with the spine as straight as is comfortable. Let your eyes softly close. Let your body become relaxed. *Pause*. Become aware that life is breathing you. Feel gratitude for that rhythmic, life-sustaining process. *Pause*. Quiet the emotions and put aside any concerns for this period of time. Still the verbal mind (that part of you that wants to reason and name and compare things). Let the non-verbal, creative mind be alert, awake, and aware.

Lift your consciousness into the light of the Higher Self (Naphsha). Imagine there the quality of humility. *Pause*. Be aware of the quality of silence, that causes one to listen to others. *Pause*. Be aware of the quality of wisdom, that causes one to see quickly and easily the difference between needs and wants. *Pause*. Become aware of the quality of service, that motivates you to serve the needs of another. *Pause*. Allow the spirits of silence, wisdom, and service to fill your consciousness. *Pause*.

Imagine one person whose needs you truly want to meet. *Pause*. Now imagine unconditional love filling your consciousness and flowing out to this person by an act of your will. *Pause*. Now allow yourself to see this person's needs as he or she sees them. *Pause*. Drawing upon your higher wisdom, now ask if it is practical for you to meet the needs of this person. *Pause*. Allow ideas to come into your awareness of how to meet the needs of this person. *Pause*.

In your imagination, see this person's needs being met. See this person's potentials being developed and expressed. *Pause*. Imagine this person successful, joyous, happy. Feel deep gratitude that you can see these possibilities. Pause.

Now bring your consciousness back to the personal self. Be aware of your body and your environment.

At this point you may wish to make a will statement pertaining to the above experience, such as: "I will to be a humble person and to express humility in my life."

Chapter 9
THE FOURTH ATTITUDE
The Attitude of Justice and Fairness

The Fourth Attitude reads thus:

A transpersonal attitude is theirs,
those who hunger and thirst for justice and
   fairness *(kenoota)*;
they shall attain it.

Kenoota means sound, proper, right, just, equitable, fair. To hunger and thirst for something is to touch the depths of human life. If we are hungry—really hungry—all we have on our mind is food, something to alleviate the gnawing inner pain. There are numerous stories in literature of characters being so hungry they relinquished their heritage in order to get food. When we hunger and thirst for fair and just behavior we open the mind to the required insight, wisdom, and "know-how" to attain that which is right for ourselves.

Years ago I decided to meditate daily. I had meditated and prayed most of my adult life, but at irregular times. I got the notion that if I had a regular time for meditation, my inner life would become much more developed and nourishing for me. I tried meditating in the evening before retiring. I found this time unsatisfactory because I retired at varying times and in varying states of sleepiness. I tried getting up at three o'clock in the morning, when I would not be interrupted by the telephone or for other reasons. I found I was too sleepy and not as alert as I wanted to be. I next tried four o'clock in the morning, then five o'clock. Each time period worked for a little while. Then one day I decided I would meditate each day at a proper psychological time for me: an hour before my regular time for arising—but before eating breakfast, regardless of whether I got up an hour earlier or not. When I decided to put meditation before eating, it really worked! And it has worked for over a quarter of a century. When I want something as much as I want to satisfy physical needs, I find I can accomplish whatever it is.

The inner drive to know and live with justice and fairness becomes a survival issue for those who express it. Satisfying hunger and thirst are basic instinctive needs. They are essential for our existence. Perhaps those who spoke Aramaic also knew that right, sound behavior is just as essential as food and drink. We might survive without right and fair behavior, but what kind of existence would that be?

The Fourth Attitude emphasizes a deep desire or longing for an essential spiritual need. We all get what we want and desire. We are now manifesting in our lives what we have wanted in the past. Sometimes by the time our desires manifest themselves, we have changed our minds or are unable to recall what we wanted. Thus it is important to use the energy of desire for essentials. If we desire only those essentials such as food and drink, and just and right behavior, we will keep them fresh in our minds. Our need for them will be just as great when they are apparent in our lives as when we hungered for them. The deep longing mentioned in this Fourth Attitude is a longing to be in harmony with the universal Source. The creator of this rule knew that harmony with the Source can be obtained only if one's motives are pure and one's behavior is right and just.

We could therefore say that the Fourth Attitude is one of alignment, of creating a vertical relationship with the truths and attributes of the Source, and expressing these truths in our relationships with others. The Fourth Attitude conforms to the Golden Rule: "Do unto others as you would have them do unto you." Many of the world's religions have this rule in some form:

Christianity

All things whatsoever ye would that men should do to you, do ye even so to them: for this is the Law and the Prophets. (Matthew 7:12)

Judaism

What is hateful to you, do not to your fellow-men. That is the entire Law; all the rest is commentary. (Talmud, Shabbat, 31 a.)

Brahmanism

This is the sum of duty: Do naught unto others which would cause you pain if done to you. (Mahabharata 5, 1517)

Buddhism

Hurt not others in ways that you yourself would find hurtful. (Udana-Varga 5, 18)

Confucianism

Surely it is the maxim of loving-kindness: Do not unto others that you would not have them do unto you. (Analects 15, 23)

Taoism

Regard your neighbor's gain as your own gain, and your neighbor's loss as your own loss. (T'ai Shang Kan Ying P'ien)

Zoroastrianism

That nature alone is good which refrains from doing unto another whatsoever is not good for itself. (Dadistan-i-dinik 64.5)

Islam

No one of you is a believer until he desires for his brother that which he desires for himself. (Sunnah)

An Exercise in the Fourth Attitude

Find a quiet place. Sit in a chair or in a relaxed position on the floor. Relax the body, quiet the emotions, and still the personal, thinking mind. Let the creative mind be alert, awake, and aware.

Imagine the words, "Justice. Justice for all." Allow images of justice to appear on the screen of your mind. (This imaging must remain positive.) See yourself being treated justly, fairly, and equitably. Allow yourself to feel the soundness of this. Take time to feel the goodness of being treated justly, fairly, and equitably.

Now imagine that you are in a position to be just, fair, and equitable to others. Allow these images of yourself treating others with these transpersonal qualities to come onto the screen of your mind. Feel yourself in the situation. Feel the goodness of being just, fair, and equitable. Feel the rightness of this. Feel the naturalness of these transpersonal qualities.

Spend five to ten minutes experiencing these qualities. Now you may wish to visualize justice, fairness, and equality being expressed on national and international levels.

Now, after the visualization, sit quietly and write down ideas of how you can be just, fair, and equitable in some of your relationships. Be aware of your willingness to express these transpersonal qualities.

As you go about your day, look for opportunities to express justice, fairness, and equality.

A Meditation for Spiritual Alignment

Select a quiet place, sit on a chair, on a mat, or on the floor, with the eyes closed and the back as straight as is comfortable. Let the body be relaxed. Become aware of your breathing. Be conscious that life is breathing you. Feel gratitude for that.

Read or speak this statement: *I will to align myself with the Source of life.*

Imagine a time when you longed for a drink of water, and then you had that water to drink. Imagine how good it felt to be refreshed by the water.

Now imagine the all-wise part of you—the spiritual part—that longs to align itself with the Source of your life. Imagine that the Source knows all about you, your potentials, your talents, and your abilities.

Allow this energy to surround and fill and nourish you. Feel deep gratitude that the all-wise part of you hungers and thirsts for this loving nurturing energy and can attain it by being willing to thirst and hunger for it. Rest in the energy of fulfillment of your need.

When you feel ready, become aware of your breathing, aware of your body, and aware of how you are sitting. Be aware of the room. Gently open your eyes. You are now ready to go about your life, knowing your spiritual hunger and thirst can be satisfied.

Chapter 10

THE FIFTH ATTITUDE
The Attitude of Unconditional Love

The Fifth Attitude reads thus:

A transpersonal attitude is theirs,
those whose love is without conditions *(khooba);*
they will therefore receive unconditional love
(rakhma).

Unconditional love is the quintessential positive attitude underlying and tying together the other seven attitudes. Unconditional love is an active, moving, transpersonal energy.

Because of its transpersonal qualities, unconditional love opens the heart-center. The unfolding of the heart-center is marked by our capacity to express compassion, understanding, and a deep desire to serve. During times of suffering and seeing others suffer, the heart is touched at a deep level. We are able to take action because we can identify with the ones who are suffering. Each of us, at anytime, can take action to express unconditional love, but all too often it takes a catastrophe to open our heart-center.

Some children were swimming at a lake, and one child went out too far. He was on the verge of drowning when a group of men came around the curve. One man quickly jumped into the water and brought the child to shore. He worked diligently and lovingly to force the water out of the child's lungs, saving his life.

The man was a member of the local school

board. He had failed to realize that he could rescue many children through his power to effect equal educational opportunities. His heart had not been touched so deeply until he saw a helpless child drowning. Not until the catastrophic moment was he able to identify with a child of a different race. Fortunately, the heart often does not shut back down after such an incident, but can remain compassionate and open to unconditional love. After that incident the man had a deep desire to look at other areas of his life to see how he could open his heart more, and his position on the school board seemed a logical place to effect his newly discovered desire to take action without racial discrimination.

Sensitivity is one of the qualities that comes with opening the heart-center—we become more sensitive to the needs of others. Unconditional love expresses itself in cooperation and goodwill towards all. It is an all-inclusive love—no one is excluded. Those who hold the attitude of unconditional love are concerned with preventing harm, of living in a state of harmlessness. Their motives and actions express goodwill.

The attitude of unconditional love involves actively helping, while expressing tenderness, compassionate understanding, unselfish intent, and wise judgment. It is free from any wish for regard or recognition for such acts.

In *The Voice of the Silence*, H.P. Blavatsky expresses this well:

Let thy Soul lend its ear to every cry of pain like as the lotus bares its heart to drink the morning sun.

Let not the fierce sun dry one tear of pain before thyself has wiped it from the sufferer's eye.

But let each burning human tear drop on thy heart and there remain; nor ever brush it off until the pain that caused it is removed.

These tears, O thou of heart most merciful, these are the streams that irrigate the fields of charity immortal.

Unconditional love does not mean keeping the object of our love happy and comfortable on a personality level. It means using foresight and wisdom to keep alive those qualities which will stimulate the growth and well-being of our loved ones. Love guards, stimulates, and protects, yet it does not hinder freedom. Unconditional love engenders a sense of personal responsibility.

Unconditional love is expressed and experienced on all four levels of our being. On a physical level, unconditional love is a lightness, a sense of relief, a warmth which is often felt in the chest and throat—we feel relaxed and free of tensions.

On an emotional level, we feel unconditional love as a sense of freedom, non-defensiveness, and joy. We feel open and responsive. We have a sense of well-being. We have a feeling of liking ourselves—our self-esteem is at optimum and we highly regard others.

On a mental level, we are accepting and able to understand all points of view without blame and judgment. We feel free to express our beliefs and our opinions because we are not attached to our ideas. We give others the freedom to express their ideas and opinions and we seek to understand them without pre-judgment.

On a spiritual level, we experience unconditional love as a sense of positive creative energy. We feel compassion and a desire to give and relate to others and to unite with them. We feel trust and a deep inner security of knowing that, for self and others, all is well. We are able to relate to all people with a warm acceptance and with outgoing goodwill.

The attitude of unconditional love is essential to the Law of Attitudes, referred to earlier as a prerequisite to the *Code of Conduct*. Chapter 14 is devoted to the practice of unconditional love—a powerful means of harmony, joy, and vitality in our lives.

An Exercise to Develop the Qualities of Unconditional Love

The following qualities may be used in various ways. Select a quality. Use it daily for one week. Post the word where you can see it often—on your bulletin board, mirror, or on the wall. Look up the meaning of the word in the dictionary. You can use it in a meditation by visualizing yourself expressing the quality in your daily life. Ponder the word and its meaning. After you have used all the qualities for one week each, then you could use them for longer periods—two weeks, or a month—personalizing the quality in your life. You may wish to write your experiences in your personal journal.

Qualities for Special Focus

Humility
Patience
Sympathy
Persistence
Humor
Joy

Compassion
Wisdom
Acceptance
Tolerance
Forgiveness
Service

Chapter 11

THE SIXTH ATTITUDE
The Attitude that Allows Us to See the Source

The Sixth Attitude reads thus:

A transpersonal attitude is theirs,
those without faults *(dadcean)* in their minds
   (libhoun);
they will see the Source *(Alaha)*.

Cean means pure, clean, sound, free of fault.
The prefix *dad* means complete, entire. The
Sixth Attitude is a transpersonal one that completely purifies our consciousness and removes
faults and illusions. It enables us to see life and
circumstances as they are—without prejudices,
feelings of insecurity, fear of lack, illness, or
inadequacies.

Our personal self tends to be concerned about
the future and holds onto the past; it worries
about what we did not do, or what we should
have done, or what we should have left undone.
The only time we can change anything is in the
present. The present moment is *our opportunity to
choose.* We can stay in the consciousness of the
personal self—the "little" self—or raise our
consciousness into the transpersonal (above the
personal) self. In the transpersonal level of
consciousness, we are not limited by the faults in
our minds, and therefore we are not limited in
our thinking. We can see the Source of life, as
set forth by the Essenes.

The personal self tends not to think of our

potential, of what is possible for us to experience. Just imagine, if you can, a mind that is *complete,* one that is *total, whole, without blemish or fault.* Imagine a mind that is all-inclusive. By inclusive I mean completely open to all—to all there is, to everyone and everything! If we could allow ourselves to see the Source of life, we could comprehend the universe as its Creator does—we could conceive universal principles. The Source, or Creator, as used in this text, is translated from the Aramaic word *Alaha,* which means the highest of the high. The Source means the source of all life.

One whose mind is completely without flaw is so pure and whole that he or she can be in touch with and aware of the Source. The mystery of the laws of nature are understandable to one whose mind is pure and without fault. That person has a cosmic view of life. Such was the goal of the Essenes: to know all that was knowable to them. They strove to free their minds of faults and preserved the *Code of Conduct* so we, too, could attain purity of vision.

This Source is unknowable to those who have flaws or faults in their minds, or to those who have divided minds. When the mind is whole (healthy), not divided or clouded with illusion, that which was previously considered unknowable becomes knowable.

Thomas A. Edison put his whole mind into the search for the law that governed electricity. No doubt he perceived the law readily, but he performed experiment after experiment to discover how to harness it for our use. Why did he not give up after the first thousand experiments? Because he *knew*. He *saw* how this creative energy from the Source could be used to light the world. That vision would not let him stop. We now have electricity because his mind was undivided, unclouded, and was free to comprehend an aspect of the Source.

When we are negative, in a low state of mind, or have a poor attitude, we cannot see our potential, or that of others, or of a situation. We are closed to *possibility thinking*. For example, when we are depressed we don't even seek a way out of the depression. We cannot perceive the possibility of a positive solution. If we do not know how to be in charge of our attitudes we often allow illusions and distortions to cloud our minds and, in so doing, we block the creative force which is available to each of us.

The Sixth Attitude refers to how we function when we are at one with our transpersonal self (Naphsha): we see things whole. We elevate ourselves to a state of joy, of deep gratitude or serenity, and let go of the limitations once perceived as real. These illusions no longer hide the facts from our awareness. Imagine seeing the world as the Creator sees it! A universal point of view enables us to see life in perspective.

Our evaluations of our past events and experiences form, and sometimes limit, our belief systems. Belief systems contain facts, ideas, symbols, images, expectations, and so forth. Because we can remember how the past has been, we sometimes project it onto the future. We create future expectations based on the past—which can keep us from appreciating present possibilities. The past is gone; we have only our memory of how we thought it was. We do not have the future because it has not yet happened. All we do have is the present. Peace of mind cannot be found in the past or in the future—it is now. The Essenes spent their time neither in the past nor in the future, but lived in the present. They looked neither backward nor forward, but upward to the part of them that knew and could be in touch with "the raincloud of knowable things"—information available to those who seek the mysteries of life.

There are those who can see the Source in nature's laws and in life's events. The Essenes specialized in both methods: they found directions for living in peace within themselves and within the community. With a pure, wholly clean mind, we can see life the way it is. We are all responsible for our attitudes and our well-being. The creative force of love is available to us all.

Meditation for Seeing Life Whole

This meditation can be used for situations, relationships, or to attain the truth about something you are seeking to know.

Select a quiet place, sit on a chair, a mat, or on the floor, with your back as straight as comfortable. Let your eyes close softly. Become aware of your breathing. Be aware that life is breathing you.

Quiet your emotions, still the concrete, thinking mind. Be aware of the Sixth Attitude, which enables you to see the Source of life.

Raise your consciousness to your Naphsha, above your head. Imagine it as a center of light energy—a place where you are all-wise and perfect.

In this light create an image of yourself whole, in perfect health, filled with joy and gladness. Imagine yourself in this state of wholeness, doing some kind of service for others. This may be something you have never done. Imagine yourself doing it happily and easily, with joy. Hold this picture and allow this joy to express itself through your body. Retain this image in the light of the Naphsha for three to five minutes.

Now just let the image go. Become aware of your body. Become aware of your breathing and where you are sitting. When you are ready, open your eyes and return to your usual activities.

Chapter 12
THE SEVENTH ATTITUDE
The Attitude of the Peace Server

The Seventh Attitude reads thus:

A transpersonal attitude is theirs,
those serving *(abdey)* the Peace of the Creator
  (Shlama);
they will be called the heirs of the Source
  (Alaha).

Abdey is a verb which means to serve with
effect, to work effectively or productively by
offering service. By serving the peace of the
Creator, we acquire a transpersonal attitude that
allows us to promote and protect the harmony
desired by the Creator. *Shlama* means tranquil-
ity—a peace, a serenity that is under and in
accordance with the will of the Source. Our task
is to extend to individuals the peace which exists
with the Source of creation. By being at one with
this ultimate peace we can effectively serve the
great need to bring peace into the consciousness
of humanity. By becoming peacemakers or peace
creators—first by being a center of peace ourselves and serving others by extending that
harmony to them—we become inheritors of the
Source.

This attitude is somewhat different from most
of the other attitudes in that it requires a task or
an act of service to be performed. To render such
service requires a special transpersonal attitude,
the Attitude of Peace. The following fable,

whose author is unknown, shares the secret of becoming a peacemaker:

The Secret of Peace

There is a story of an ancient king, by nature peaceful, merciful and kind, who was beset by his neighbor-king, intent on war and conquest. The peaceful king sent an envoy to the warlike neighbor, proposing peaceful terms. Meantime, he ordered his people to begin protective measures in the event of war. Their hearts were heavy with fear and sorrow.

The king prayed steadfastly for some means of bringing about a peaceful solution. One day the wife of a courtier came to him and asked permission to reveal a secret to him. She whispered something in his ear which made him smile. Then he told her to go and seek out other women in the city, confide her secret to each one, and let the news of it spread throughout the city and the land. The king then went to his own wife, told her the secret, and she also went abroad in the land, imparting this great secret to the women she met. So from end to end of this kingdom, as the women traveled and whispered their message to one another, a song of joy was heard and smiles returned to the people's faces.

On a certain day, word came from the envoy to the warlike king that a peace treaty had been signed. The peaceful king ordered the people to cease all preparations for war and to return to peaceful pursuits. He was told that they already had done so and that this was the reason for the widespread joy and happiness. When the courtiers demanded to know the reason for this miraculous change, the king revealed the secret each woman had whispered to another: "Every day, retire for a short period of silence; go within; pray to God, but do not pray for peace. Do not pray to God for anything at all—just sit in silence and *find* peace within yourself; and do this every day."

This was the great secret that restored joy and peace between the two kingdoms. Every effective service, wherever it may be delivered, requires a specific attitude. Peace is not the positive result of having fought and won a battle, but rather is the opening of a gate within us through which unconditional love can flow. Where there is peace, there is no anxiety. Happy are the peacemakers.

To be a peacemaker, serve yourself and others. When you become aware that you are not at peace within yourself, find the cause of the disharmony or lack of peace. Internal conflicts occur at various times. For example, a young woman had a conflict about allowing her daughter to participate in a school activity. She wanted the child to participate with her playmates, but felt anxious and apprehensive about the girl's physical welfare and the influence her friends might have on her. The mother sat down and quieted her emotions. She experienced unconditional love for the Source and for her child. She felt gratitude for the universal laws that register anxiety within her when all is not at peace. She lifted her mind into a transpersonal state. Then she became fully aware of the conflict. She became aware that if her child entered into the questioned activity, she herself would need to prepare her child for the event. She saw that her anxiety was a way of warning her to prepare her child. The mother was now clearly aware of what she needed to do and was willing to do it. In fact, if she did not prepare her child, there would indeed be further disharmony and lack of peace.

When we are at peace within ourselves, we are able to see various points of view. We can see the harmonious way, the way of peace for ourselves and others.

An Exercise in Creating Peace Within

This exercise may be used whenever you feel anxiety, concern, or indecision.

Sit quietly on a chair or on the floor in a relaxed position. Breathe deeply and quietly. Close the eyes. Relax the body, still the emotions, and quiet the mind. Reach up in consciousness to your Higher Self (Naphsha) and there contact the quality of peace. Imagine peace. Let that peace flow into your mind, your emotions, and into your body. Imagine a quiet, peaceful lake. Be aware of the calm surface of the water. Now imagine your body, mind, and emotions being calm like this beautiful peaceful lake. Let that peace pervade your consciousness. Rest in that peace.

Now get in touch with your will. Examine your willingness to make the decision that is right for you. Be aware now that you are above the anxiety and concerns. Ask within yourself, "What is the message the anxiety has for me?" Ask any question that is appropriate for you at this time. Wait for the answer to come. This is not a mental process—do not try to think out the answer. If you are using a mental process, reach higher in your consciousness. Allow the answer to come from your Naphsha, which is located above your head. Then, when you feel perfectly at peace and have the answers to your questions, be aware of your body and open your eyes. Go about your duties, taking with you the Attitude of Peace.

Chapter 13

THE EIGHTH ATTITUDE
The Attitude of Justice and Righteous Behavior

The Eighth Attitude reads thus:

A transpersonal attitude is theirs,
those being scorned and harrassed *(radpean)*
and having evil spoken against them *(bildbabon)*
because of their stand for justice and right
    behavior;
theirs is one of complete inner peace and
    serenity.

The word *radpean* means harrassment, insult, derogation of another as contemptible and unworthy of respect. *Bildbabon* means injurious, adverse, hostile. These are strongly negative feelings and actions.

Under such ridicule and adversity we require a particular set of attitudes in order to persevere in our sound behavior. Such ridicule usually causes tension, and the mind will tend to abandon the sound behavior and positive attitude in an effort to find relief from the tension.

A person continuing his "right behavior" under ridicule would by definition be free from any tension related to it. One who maintains the attitude of love for another despite being scorned and harrassed by him is practicing the attitude of having love for self, others, and the Source. This person really knows who he or she is and is free from dependence on the opinions of others. This person is not distracted by taunts and jeers, but holds the positive attitude in the light of the Higher Self (Naphsha).

When we truly identify with the Naphsha, we have a strong inner assurance of our own beingness. By having such a secure identification we can easily express transpersonal energies and qualities such as serenity, peace, joy, humor, patience, and empathy. It is a real test of our ability to maintain love for another despite his tormenting actions. We would necessarily have to hold the attitude of love for our own true Self and for the Source, who allows all others to conduct their lives as they please.

If, under ridicule, you experience tension because of your sound behavior, you may need to re-establish the Attitude of Unconditional Love. To do this, restate the Law of Attitudes and reconfirm your will to maintain these attitudes comfortably. If you maintain the attitudes as they should be, you will achieve freedom from tension while under attack. Your reward will be the experience of complete inner peace and serenity.

Transpersonal refers to a higher order, an elevated state, a state above the physical, emotional, or personal levels of functioning. When we are functioning on the transpersonal level we would perhaps be able to see and understand the cause behind another's negative action. Love for the Source, others, and self insulates the mind from receiving emotional pain when under criticism for just behavior.

Experiencing anger and hurt under criticism

indicates a failure to conform to the Law of Attitudes. To be insulated by unconditional love is not an escape or an "ivory tower" position. It is a way of rising above personal hurt on the mental, emotional, and even physical levels.

When we choose the way of right behavior—the way of living in the attitude of love in the transpersonal state—we may sometimes be misunderstood by others. This may be expressed as jealousy or fear or undue criticism. The person with right behavior is often ridiculed or attacked. Gandhi and Martin Luther King, Jr. are examples. What were their attitudes about those who scorned and harrassed them? Each of these great men had a cause: to free people. Their cause was greater than any harrassment, scorn, or ridicule, and they found infinite energy to fulfill their goals.

If this attitude of love for a tormentor is difficult to understand, it may have something to do with our level of consciousness. If we are on a personal-self level, we may find it almost impossible to "keep cool" and stay in a loving space. By elevating our consciousness to a transpersonal level, we are better able to remain objective and impersonal. From this transpersonal place we often are able to understand that the tormentors are truly the tormented ones, not us. They are striking out of their own pain and agony; we are simply the recipient of their projections. They lack the connection with their Higher Self and thus block themselves from the transpersonal energies that can comfort and enlighten them.

An Exercise to Prepare for Times of Tension

This exercise may be used when under tension, or when life seems difficult. Practice the following affirmation regularly when life is easy and smooth so that when things are difficult you can reaffirm it silently. It is most effective, however, when said aloud.

> AFFIRM: I am the *Self!* I have *choice.* I am in charge of my self, my actions, and my emotions. I now choose to be calm and serene. I am the Self. I am in charge.

Imagine you are looking at a scene, as on a television, of yourself in a situation where everyone is tense, impatient, and critical—you remain calm and serene.

Now imagine being in that scene. Be aware of the impatience and tension of others around you while you remain calm and serene. Imagine saying within yourself, "I am the Self. I have a choice. I can choose to be calm and serene or I can be like those around me. I am the Self. I have choice. I choose to be calm, serene, and in charge of myself."

The Essenes actually practiced these Eight Attitudes. Understanding these attitudes gives us insight into how the Essenes were able to live in peace when their neighbors in surrounding communities were at war. Practicing these attitudes gives us the strength and inner serenity to move peacefully and purposefully through our own lives in today's world. When the transpersonal attitudes are set in the mind by the will, we can align ourselves with the heavenly dignity and function with the will of the Source.

Part
Three

Chapter 14

UNCONDITIONAL LOVE

Jane

Jane, a woman of forty-two in my class, was beside herself with worry and concern for her eighteen-year-old daughter. Jane had had no contact with Sadie for over a month. One of Sadie's friends had just called and told Jane that Sadie was on drugs, was drinking heavily, and was "sleeping around."

Sadie was supposed to be living with her father and Jane had expected him to be providing parental guidance. Jane called her ex-husband, hoping he'd say Sadie was okay. Instead, he said he had not seen her for some time and did not know how to contact her. "She only calls when she wants money," he said.

Jane wrung her hands and wept, "If only I could see her and talk to her. Oh, what shall I do?" She feared the worst. "What shall I do?"

"Love her," I responded. "All you can do now is love her unconditionally, as you did when she was a baby. You expected nothing of her then. You just loved her. You have no control over her now. All you can do is accept her as she is, without expectation that she will be the way you want her to be. Cancel all demands you have of her. Just concentrate on your love for her."

With help, Jane was able to put aside everything except love for Sadie. One by one, she cancelled the expectations, demands, and conditions she had held. She accepted Sadie just as she was, addictions and all, and doing so, reported feelings of relief and joy, and a lightness in her body in place of the heaviness and concern she had felt.

Within days, Sadie telephoned. (This is not unusual. It quite often happens after an experience of unconditional love and forgiveness towards another.) They talked more than they had in months. Sadie seemed different and Jane related to her differently. When Jane invited Sadie for a visit, she accepted.

Jane felt a deep gladness at their reunion. Instead of telling Sadie that her life was ruined and that she looked terrible, as she would have done in the past, she focused her thoughts and feelings on loving Sadie. When Sadie talked, Jane listened. She didn't criticize or lay down rules. She realized how much they both had changed.

The new relationship between mother and daughter continued to grow. They spoke more often and occasionally had dinner together. As Sadie's trust grew, she became less resistant to Jane. After a few months she accepted Jane's suggestion to enter a drug treatment program to recover from her addictions. Unconditional love helped Jane in her struggle to guide her daughter to healthful life choices. Sadie is now making excellent grades in college and is planning to become a psychologist.

Rakhma and Khooba Love

In the Aramaic language, unconditional love is expressed with two words, *rakhma* and *khooba*. *Rakhma* means transpersonal love, a love without conditions, without requests, without demands for rewards or returns. This is love given freely. It is an impersonal love, expressed in decisions and actions. It is known as *agape* in Greek.

Khooba means pure love which includes reason, discernment, thought, and perception. It perceives what is good, wholesome, and lovable about self, others, and situations. Khooba love is an attitude that can be expressed on the thought level. When we have khooba love we readily perceive and respond to the positive qualities in another. We can see another's potential as well as our own. When we have khooba love, the mind focuses only on the positive images stored in memory rather than the negative. Khooba is a transpersonal, perceptual love. Without it, the mind cannot experience any of the transpersonal attitudes. Experiencing khooba love enables us to have a feeling of affection and warmth towards others.

The difference between these two concepts might be likened to the difference between having an intention (khooba) and carrying it out (rakhma). Khooba love is the foundation upon which rakhma acts. Both forms helped Jane in her relationship with her daughter—by unblocking the flow of love and by suggesting a positive course of action.

I recently visited a therapist friend who complained of feeling non-productive. He had become bored with orthodox psychotherapy and had retired. Then he told me of some therapy he had done a few years earlier with a prison inmate. He had greatly helped this client by using his intuition. I pointed out that perhaps he would feel differently about psychotherapy if he could work more intuitively.

I suggested he work with a professional support group whose members use intuition. I emphasized the positive qualities I saw in him—how he likes to help people, how he enjoys it when others show an interest in growing and in improving their lives. My friend soon thought of an intuitive therapist in his city who respected him and his ideas. Before we parted he was enthusiastic about his plan to contact this therapist. He was back in touch with his own positive qualities.

Khooba love enabled me to perceive the positive qualities in my friend. Rakhma love took action by suggesting a professional group for him.

Unconditional love is openness. It is an all-inclusive openness, an openness to the good in ourselves and others. The attitude of unconditional love, translated into goals, becomes the seeking of the good.

However, sometimes we tend to add conditions—a bargaining stance—such as, "I will be open to the good in the Source if the Source answers my prayers and desires. If the Source doesn't grant my wishes or give me what I want, I will withdraw my openness (love) because the Source has failed my test."

We may do a similar thing with others: "I will be open to the good in my neighbor as long as he treats me with respect. If he stops treating me with respect, he will have failed my test, and I will withdraw my openness to the good in him."

We may put conditions on ourselves as well: "I will be open to the good in myself only when I'm successful. If I fail, then I will have failed my test for me, and I will withdraw my openness to the good in myself."

When our conditions, demands, or requirements are not met, we sometimes tend to withdraw the attitude of openness and allow irritation and hostility to prevail. Sometimes we cultivate the attitude of hostility in order to feel strong, to have the energy to deal with situations. This strength may feel so good that we entertain the feeling of hostility for a long time.

When our expectations or demands are met, we may feel as if we've experienced love. What we are most likely experiencing is an illusion of openness from a temporary sense of personal satisfaction. This false sense of openness is once again threatened whenever an expectation is not met.

Unconditional love allows no condition or limitation to remain between our love of the Source, self and another. Each individual is responsible for keeping the attitude of love for the Source, the self, and others, regardless of circumstances. This requires the willingness to cancel the conditions, demands, and expectations which are perceived as causing the loss of love.

When we lose the attitude of unconditional love, we lose it because we are imposing conditions or demands on ourselves, the Source, or others. We are using our will to go contrary to the law of the Source. This is an occasion for exercising forgiveness—withdrawing our demands and reestablishing unconditional love. Being open again, we can then realistically assess the situation and choose a more appropriate course of action.

To keep our homes clean and inviting, we use vacuum cleaners to eliminate dust, lint, sand, and dirt. Unconditional love and forgiveness serve the same purpose for us—to vacuum up resentments, irritations, disgust, and other negative attitudes (while they are small and easily managed) so we can live in harmony with natural law.

How do we know what unfulfilled conditions, expectations, or demands we have placed on ourselves, others, or the Source? The following story demonstrates a process of identifying the causes of disharmony. This story also previews the process of forgiveness or "cancelling," discussed in the next chapter.

My husband and I were driving home to Los Angeles from Utah. It was necessary for us to stop in Las Vegas for the night; it was about 6:00 P.M. when we were nearing the city. I have never felt an affinity for Las Vegas, and I can feel its atmosphere miles away.

We began to discuss where we would stay and what we would do that evening. It seemed that every time I made a suggestion, my husband had another one that didn't please me. I began to get a severe headache. I felt I was picking up the Las Vegas "vibes." My headache grew worse as we drove into the city. By this time I had given up any ideas I had for the evening and was massaging my head to ease the pain. We decided on a motel, and my husband went inside to check it out.

As I sat in the car I began to think of our conversation. I realized I was out of harmony. However, I could not see what the problem was. I did not like feeling such disharmony. I thought about how understanding my husband usually is and about the things I appreciate about him. My head was still pounding. I decided to go through a forgiveness exercise because of the disharmony I felt. I did not see what demands and expectations I was putting on him or myself. I thought to myself, "I'll just say what comes to me."

While my husband was still in the motel, I closed my eyes to become more aware of my inner feelings as I sat in the car. I said aloud, "Paul Stauffer, I would prefer that you would be perfect; that you would know exactly what I want to do, even if I don't. I would prefer that you would listen to me and hear what I say and let me know you are listening. Even though you are not perfect, you don't always know what I want, and you do not always listen to me, I now cancel the expectation that you be perfect. I cancel the expectation that you know what I want to do, and I cancel the expectation that you listen to me. I accept you just as you are, and I send my unconditional love out to you."

I felt my love flowing out to him; I felt much love and appreciation for all the many things he usually does to make me comfortable and happy. My headache began to ease. I opened my eyes, looked towards the motel, and saw Paul leaving the building. By the time he reached the car, my head was comfortable.

We had a delightful evening. I did not tell Paul about the forgiveness experience because it was all my "stuff" anyway. I believe, however, that he knew on some level that he had a "different wife" from the one with whom he drove into the city. I did not realize that I had expected him to be perfect and that I had put so many other expectations on him. I did, however, express my unconditional love and appreciation to him directly for his understanding and consideration.

When we block our love from another person we feel our energy shut down. The energy stops flowing to the other person and at the same time energy from our Naphsha stops flowing into us. We are short-circuited. As soon as harmony is restored, the healing energy starts flowing into the self from the Naphsha and out to the other person.

My headache was no doubt caused by the lack of energy flow. I had broken the law of attitudes. I had shut myself off from Naphsha, my source of healing energy, and in so doing, I blocked my love from my husband.

When we discover that we are out of harmony and are willing to do anything necessary to restore the harmony again, we can help ourselves to health.

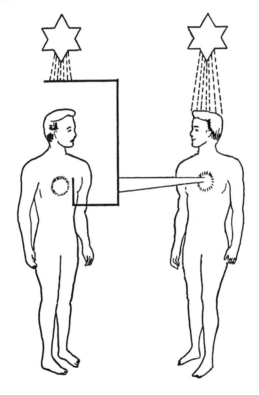

When we block our love for another, we block the energy from our own Naphsha.

Jake

All living things respond to love or the absence of it. Plants, animals, and certainly human beings respond in a positive way to love and acceptance. They also suffer from the lack of it.

"One of your clients swore that you could help me," declared Jake, a forty-year-old horse trainer. Two years before, he had had a beautiful stallion that he was training for horse shows. He was attempting to teach this horse a special maneuver and the horse threw him off. "It didn't injure me," he said, "it just hurt my pride. After that, every time I would get on him he would throw me. I was so angry at him, I castrated him. Then he lost his spirit. So we both lost."

He decided to get another horse. He looked everywhere until finally, at a horse show in Holland, he saw a beautiful, spirited stallion. He knew he just had to have him. He had the horse shipped to California and had been training him for about six months when one day the stallion threw him. He decided not to ride him again until he learned what to do to prevent this from recurring.

I asked him what his attitude was towards the horse.

"I'm mad at him. I'm mad that he's in charge."

I explained to him that the horse can only be won by love. I told him about khooba love, the ability to see the good in another or in situations. Then I asked him what was good about the horse.

"He is full of spirit, he is beautiful, he is healthy and strong, and he can respond to my training."

I directed him in a visualization exercise in which he felt unconditionally loving towards his horse. In this visualization, the horse was responding in a positive way to his direction. I asked him to visualize every day a loving partnership in which he was in charge and the horse lovingly responded to him. I suggested he feel love and appreciation for his horse and his fine qualities.

"Thanks—unconditional love is working for me and my horse," was written in a note I later received from Jake.

Anger

Anger is an immediate and automatic emotional response. When we feel that we (or others) are being treated disrespectfully, unjustly, shamefully, or inhumanely, anger floods in. A great charge of energy is released through the adrenal glands and is expressed through the physical body and the emotions. This heightened energy prepares the body to fight or to run for safety. It must be used or discharged from the body and not allowed to accumulate.

If used appropriately, this surge of energy is channeled to correct injustice, indignities, and cruelty. However, a person unable to release anger appropriately is blocking love. Hatred is a hardened form of unreleased anger which is most destructive to health. If we use this energy of anger to reciprocate in kind—to inflict cruelty or pain—then we are lowering ourselves to the level of our persecutors. The dynamic energy of anger can be better used to lift ourselves and others to more creative solutions.

One way of releasing anger is to verbalize it. Give it a voice! Imagine that these deep, angry feelings can speak, and allow them to express the hurt or humiliation. This method is especially recommended if you have been treated violently—find a private place with freedom to yell and scream out the anger and pain. After such a release, the next step is to raise your consciousness from the emotional to the mental level. Assess the situation and see how you can use that powerful energy to bring about change.

When we hold the attitude of anger and hostility we tend to be closed to the good in a situation, in others, or in self. We do not see the whole picture or the possibility of positive solutions. The phrase, "He was so angry he couldn't see straight," conveys this dynamic. When hostility directs our goal we usually want to do harm and say unkind and critical things about self or others. We are "cued" to see only the negative.

The attitude of hostility is as much a disregard for the Law of Attitudes as stepping out of a third-floor window is a disregard for the Law of

Gravity. To close ourselves to the good in others and self is as foolish as going into a grocery store, selecting the poorest apples we can find, paying for them, and then getting upset and angry that the store sold us bad apples.

We can choose the kinds of apples we want and we can choose the kinds of attitudes we want. We can choose to perceive the good qualities in our neighbor or the poor qualities. Our neighbor doesn't "make us" choose hostility any more than the store makes us select bad apples. We can, and do, choose which attitude to emphasize: the attitude of love, of being open to all and looking for the good; or the attitude of hostility, of being blind to the good and attending only to the bad.

Being open to the good does not mean we have to be unaware of that which is not good. It is possible to select the sound apples while being aware of the decaying ones. It is possible to emphasize the good qualities of our neighbor while being aware of his deficiencies. It is possible to see his good intentions as well as his errors.

Focusing on the good is more profitable. Being open to the good enables us to see when there is a lack of good. It opens us to both the good and its absence and thus allows us to be more realistic in choosing appropriate actions. Choosing to focus on the good enables us to be more effective in our relationships. The fact that we make the choice is of great importance—we are taking action by exercising our ability to love.

To be unconditionally loving and forgiving is a way of viewing life. Unconditional love allows no condition or limitation to remain between our love of self and another. In the next chapter we will examine the process of forgiveness, of cancelling expectations and conditions that block the attitude of love.

Chapter 15
FORGIVENESS
The Cancelling Machine

Fred

"I'm so angry I'm afraid I'll kill someone! I just have to do something with my anger."

"When did all this anger start?" I asked Fred, a well-built eighteen-year-old college sophomore. His face was flushed and he clenched his fists as he spoke.

"It all started when I was seven. We lived next door to a family of three boys my age. I could outrun all of them. I could beat them at all the games we played. That made them mad at me and they ridiculed me and made fun of me. That would make me so mad," he said, gritting his teeth.

"I wanted to beat them up. When I did that, all three of them jumped on me and beat me up. That made me so frustrated and angry. I just wanted to kill all of them. I thought of ways I could do this. I have visualized and imagined that for years, even after we moved away. Every time I think of them I want to destroy them. Now I project that out to other people."

"Like who?" I asked.

"People in traffic and when I play rugby, a game I love and have played for years."

The next week Fred came in for his appointment, his face and hands all bruised, saying, "I've just got to stop all this anger."

"What happened to you?" I asked.

"On Saturday night I really made an ass of myself. I got in a fight and took on two guys bigger than I am and I picked one up and threw him down a long flight of stairs. He went all the way down, too!"

"Did he get hurt?" I asked.

"I don't know; I haven't found out yet."

We discussed how he would feel if this young fellow was seriously hurt or died. Big tears ran down his bruised cheeks.

"I don't really want to kill anyone but I just feel like it at times."

Then he told me that he had given up rugby because he feared he would hurt someone seriously.

I pointed out to him that the neighbor boys had not ridiculed him in eight or nine years and he was still carrying on as though it had happened yesterday. I told him he could re-program his conscious and unconscious mind to love and give life to himself and others, which would flush out all the hate and anger he had been feeling. He was eager to learn how to do this.

I asked him to close his eyes and imagine the three little boys sitting on my couch and to imagine seeing them just as they were ten years before. Then I asked him to tell them what he would have preferred they had done when they played together. He said, "I would have preferred that you had just accepted me as I was, but you didn't do that."

"Tell them how *tired* you are of hating them."

He told them he was tired of hating them and he wanted to quit and get all the anger out of his system. Then he was able to say, with conviction, that he cancelled the expectation that they be different than they were.

I then told him that there was a part of him, a spiritual part, that could unconditionally love and forgive—the part of him that gave up rugby because he did not want to hurt someone; the part that felt sorrow if he had hurt the young man. I asked him to reach up in consciousness to a center of love and light above his head and imagine that light and love filling him with unconditional love. Then I asked him to send that love out to the three little boys. He was able to do that. He was able to feel real love for them.

He reported that he felt his chest loosen and he felt warmth around his heart. His face was aglow—he was amazed that he could feel such relief.

I had instructed him to get in touch with his spiritual part and to bring its love and light down into his body, to flush out the hate and anger. He learned how to use his will to change the pattern of destruction to one of expressing love.

This story illustrates how Fred was able to cancel the expectations, demands, and conditions that caused him to carry on a program of hate and anger. We cannot hate another without lowering our own self-esteem. This young man put himself in dangerous situations—it looked as though he was trying to destroy himself. I feel strongly that the value we put on another is the value we put on ourselves.

The concept of forgiveness illustrated in this story comes directly from the Essene *Code of Conduct*. Studying this formula carefully will help you forgive all those who offend you—even yourself!

The Code states:

> To forgive is to cancel all demands, conditions, and expectations held in your mind that block the Attitude of Love; that is to say, to cancel the conditions, demands, and expectations which prevent the mind from maintaining the Attitude of Love.

The Aramaic word for forgive is "cancel." What is to be cancelled by an act of forgiveness? Answer: that factor in our mind which blocks love. Forgiving is both mental and spiritual—it involves the will and the mind. *It does not depend on any external circumstances.* The expectation, demand, or condition is cancelled in our own mind. Therefore, forgiveness requires that we be aware of the error of withdrawing love from another. There must be a *willingness* to correct this error in order to restore inner harmony. Requiring another to do certain things—"he ought to do this;" "she should do that"—in order to receive our love is conditional love and is in error according to the Essene *Code of Conduct*.

Cancelling is not the same as pardoning, condoning, or approving. It does not wipe out the wrong of another. We cannot cancel another's action or another's error. Forgetting or clearing the memory of the wrong is not cancelling. Cancelling is the dropping or removing of the *requirement* that the other person perform in any certain way in order to be loved.

Forgiveness is a natural, normal process when we hold the attitude of unconditional love. Unconditional love and forgiveness fit like hand and glove. We cannot have unconditional love and be unforgiving. Forgiveness is contingent upon a loving, totally accepting attitude.

Joe

Joe, the father of four children, sat in the front row at a three-hour workshop, taking in every word. He was so eager to learn that he asked many questions and took copious notes.

At the last session he said, "I really need help." He told us that he had come to the conference alone. His wife and two daughters were attending a Girl Scout camp. He hesitated, then said, "We had two sons, but about six weeks ago I told our fourteen-year-old that he could not ride his motor bike anymore until we had a talk and set up some rules about riding the bike safely—he had been taking chances and doing daring things on the bike. I took his key and put it in my pocket.

"The next day after school, the fourteen-year-old was complaining about not having a key to ride his bike, so my seventeen-year-old son said,

'Here's my key.' The younger son took the key and rode into the hills behind our home and killed himself in a serious accident on the bike."

There was a silence. Tears streamed down this man's face as he said, "My older son has not spoken a word since that day. He took to alcohol and drugs. He refuses to see a doctor or a counselor."

About four days after that conference I received a letter from Joe. In the letter he said, "I returned home from the conference in the afternoon, in time to go to work on the three o'clock shift. My wife and daughters were still away. When I opened the door and walked in, it looked like a cyclone had hit. The house reeked of marijuana; beer cans and wine bottles were everywhere. Everything was in shambles. I felt sick!

"I went upstairs and knocked on my son's door, hoping he was there. He finally answered, saying he didn't want to talk to me. I went to my own room and threw myself across the bed and wept. As I released my hurt, disappointment, and agony, I began to realize how much I really loved my son. At this point, nothing mattered—the marijuana, the wine, the beer, the whole mess. I was filled with unconditional love for my son. I accepted him just as he was and had been, without demanding any changes whatsoever. I loved him as I had never loved him before. I felt such a release, such an inner freedom. Joy flooded my whole being! I wept with joy. At last all the hurt and anger was gone.

I was at one with my son again.

"I looked at the clock, got up, and went downstairs and picked up my jacket. I was about to leave the house to go to work, when my son came down the stairs and threw himself into my arms. He has not stopped talking since!"

Joe stated in the letter that he wanted to take more training in unconditional love and forgiveness. "I want to teach this to my whole family."

It is surprising how really unforgiving most of us are. Many people are resentful and hateful towards inanimate objects, themselves, and others—without realizing that they are. In my work in unconditional love and forgiveness, I have found middle-aged and older adults still hating relatives or friends because of issues which occurred clear back in childhood. Often I learn that these significant others have long-since died, but the hate and resentment is just as alive and strong as when they first became destructive forces.

Why do we hang on to such resentments? The answer is that we don't know how to let go of them. Dan MacDougald said, "If we know how to forgive, we will forgive; if we don't forgive, it is because we do not know how."

I have found that most people who feel unable to forgive believe that forgiveness requires telling the other person he or she has been forgiven. Communicating that may likely add stress to an already strained relationship. Often what happens is that the person wishing to forgive does not know how he will be received by the other. Because he feels uncertain, he fails to forgive. *Forgiveness is something that happens within us.* No one is required to tell anyone anything. We simply need to be willing to let go of the anger, hostility, and bad feelings that are disrupting our life.

Forgiveness means "giving for"—giving positive, instead of negative, actions. It means giving love, understanding, and acceptance where there has been hate, resentment, and disharmony. It means changing the attitude of disappointment by cancelling expectations and allowing an attitude of unconditional love to flow out to the person who disappointed us.

I had an appointment to have lunch with a friend. I was at the meeting place a few minutes early, expecting my friend to be there to meet me. I waited fifteen minutes and he did not come. I thought of telephoning him, but decided to allow a little more time. After forty-five minutes I finally contacted him at his office. He was in the throes of many business pressures and had forgotten our appointment.

This was an excellent opportunity for me to practice forgiveness! I was very hurt and disappointed that he had forgotten the appointment.

A part of the forgiveness process sometimes consists of putting ourselves in the other person's place. In this case, I would need to understand that my friend was so harrassed that morning that he could not remember our appointment.

This is understanding, but not forgiveness. This method sometimes works with simple situations, but it will not work where there has been deep hurt or disappointment.

Forgiveness requires cancelling our expectations. The incident must be lifted from the physical and emotional levels—where problems in relationships usually occur—to higher levels. On the mental level we change the expectations into preferences. The preference states how we would have liked it to be.

I had three expectations of my friend. All three were on the physical and emotional levels. First, I expected him to be as eager to see me as I was to see him. Second, I expected him to put our appointment at the top of his priority list. Third, I expected him to keep in his mind all morning that he was having lunch with me.

The human mind is somewhat like a typewriter—it can type only one letter at a time. The mind can cancel only one expectation at a time, and that expectation must be stated clearly so the mind can fully understand the expectation and the transaction.

In my imagination I visualized my friend. I said to myself, "John, I would have preferred you to have been at the meeting place when I arrived, but you were not there. I don't want to hang on to this expectation, and tell myself things that are untrue about our relationship, and hurt myself. I now cancel the expectation which I had, that you would be there at the place waiting for me when I arrived."

Then from this mental level of stating a preference I raised my consciousness to the spiritual level, the place of the Higher Self (Naphsha). I was able at this level to allow love from the Higher Self to flow into me and heal my hurt and disappointment. I allowed this love to fill me. I sent a stream of love out to my friend. I said, "John, I send this love out to you just as you were this morning and the way you are now." Then I felt warmth, love, and compassion for John.

I took the other two expectations, one by one, and dealt with each of them in the same way. When I finished all three expectations, there was nothing between John and me except unconditional love!

You see, I could not cancel the fact that he did not meet me for lunch. What I did cancel were the expectations I had of him, which were interfering with the flow of love I had for him. Forgiveness restored that flow. I had felt emotionally hurt, and that kept me from perceiving John's intentions. The hurt I felt had blocked my love for John and allowed me to imagine that he was careless, thoughtless, or didn't want to have lunch with me.

By lifting my consciousness to a mental level and stating my expectations in the form of preferences, I found immediate relief from my hurt and the games my imagination was playing. I took my attention off John and dealt directly with my preferences. I felt some relief, but I didn't stop there. I then lifted my consciousness to the spiritual level—to my Naphsha—and again experienced love for myself, which I had shut off when I blocked my love for John. After cancelling my expectations and sending my love out to him, I was in the flow of life again. What a joy to feel the energy of love after temporarily blocking myself from it!

To forgive is to be willing to get back into the flow of life—to be willing to allow love from the Source of life, or God, to flow into us and out to that other person we need to forgive, for our own health's sake. We cannot hate and remain healthy physically, emotionally, and spiritually. Hate blocks the flow of love and life that nurtures and heals us.

The Process of Forgiveness

Forgiveness is a willingness to hold a certain attitude. It is a willingness to move forward. It is a willingness to be more comfortable and suffer less. It is a willingness to take responsibility for oneself and to allow others to take responsibility for themselves. Forgiveness is a decision *not to punish ourselves for the wrongs of others or other circumstances*. It is a decision to re-enter the flow of love and life.

STEP 1: Say to yourself: "I choose to stop punishing myself and feeling bad for what (name of person) has done or is doing."

STEP 2: Imagine that the person you need to

forgive is in front of you. You may wish to close your eyes. As you hold the image of this person in front of you, say aloud: "I would have preferred you had said (or done) _____ ."

STEP 3: Say: "But you didn't do that, so I now will to release this incident. I choose to let it go and be free of it."

STEP 4: Say: "Therefore, I cancel all demands, expectations, and conditions that you do (or say, or be) _____ in the past and now. I cancel the demand that you be (any certain way). You are totally responsible for your actions and deeds, and I release you to your own good."

STEP 5: Close your eyes and raise your consciousness into the Higher Self (Naphsha). Imagine the love that the Naphsha has for you. Feel that compassion and love from Naphsha; allow it to flow into you and release all the conditions and expectations and demands. Really feel the positive qualities of the Naphsha, that part of you that has protected, loved, and nurtured you all the days of your life.

STEP 6: With your eyes still closed, continue to feel the love from the Naphsha and now say to the person you are forgiving: "I send this love from my Naphsha out to you just as you are and have been." Feel this love flowing out from you to this person. Take your time to feel and experience this.

STEP 7: Now be aware of your body and how it feels. See if you are holding on to any demands that this person change in any way. If you do not feel release, repeat the process. Repeat the process for each action you are holding against the person. The mind cannot do a blanket forgiveness—each incident must be treated separately. Always examine your willingness to be free. If you do not find release, there may be another related incident that is not yet in your conscious mind. Ask: "Is something else blocking this process?" If so, it will usually come up immediately. Process what comes. If nothing comes, feel deep gratitude that you can feel love from your Naphsha and can send it out to the forgiven one. The sense of relief will come.

This exercise can be done often. It works for small hurts and disappointments and it works for deep emotional trauma. It works anytime we feel love is blocked.

Chapter 16
PRACTICING FORGIVENESS
Forgiveness in Families

Psychologist Abraham Maslow created a model of human behavior based on studying high achievers. In his work Maslow identified inner urges or drives responsible for behavior. He wrote:

> The basic needs of the individual are so basic that if they are not met, or in the absence of these factors, the individual will become ill. The fulfillment of these basic needs will prevent the presence of illness. To meet the needs of the individual will restore them to health or cure the illness. [1]

These basic needs encompass all facets of human existence, from the need for food to the need for truth and beauty.

Among the basic needs identified by Maslow are the important physical needs for food, shelter, and security; and the psychological needs for love and acceptance. We expect children's physical and psychological needs to be met in the home. We expect parents to love and esteem their children, to protect and nurture them, and to look forward to their unfoldment and development. Children expect, and even demand, that parents meet these obligations; they often become bitter and resentful when the parents do not.

Nevertheless, we cannot always count on parents to be mature, to perform according to these expectations—so many of them have not had their own basic needs met as children or in adulthood. In fact, parents sometimes produce children in order to satisfy their needs for love and appreciation. This may work when the children are quite young, but when they become older, they resent their parents' motives and fiercely struggle for individuality and independence.

Suppose I have a great need for a basket of apples. I know apples grow on trees. I see a beautiful, healthy tree. I expect the tree to give me apples. I see no apples, so I assume they are hidden under the leaves and branches. I look and search for apples; I demand to be given apples. None of my demands or actions bring forth apples. I simply cannot get apples from this tree because it does not have apples—it is an oak tree!

This predicament is similar to that of children who expect and demand love and caring from parents who have none to give. Sometimes husbands and wives expect love and tenderness from spouses who have little or none to give. Both are examples of looking for apples in an oak tree.

Tom

Tom, age forty, came to a workshop and said he was angry at his mother and had been for thirty-five years. He said that when he was a child, he felt lonely and uncared for, that his mother never nurtured or encouraged him. He refused to forgive her. He wanted to be angry at her as a punishment because she was selfish.

During the workshop we helped him to see what he was doing to himself with anger and resentment; how he was punishing himself instead of his mother. We pointed out how tense he becomes as he talks about his mother and his hatred of her; how his anxiety and constant anger are blocking his creativity and interfering with his fine work as an actor; and how he unintentionally projects some of these feelings onto his wife. We reminded him that his mother was not likely to change. Although neither of them could change what had happened when he was a child, he had the power to change his present reactions. He could stop hurting himself by being angry and resentful and upsetting his physical and emotional system, his marriage, and his career.

We suggested that Tom forgive his mother—to cancel the expectations he had of her. Since she had not been able to encourage and nurture him in forty years, perhaps he could just let those expectations go.

Tom decided to forgive her. He said, "Mother, I would have preferred that you had encouraged me, loved and nurtured me when I was a child, but you did not do that then or since, so I cancel these expectations. I don't want to continue to hate you and be mad at you. I see I am only hurting myself. I see I have not been nurturing to myself either. I now send my love out to you just as you were then and as you are now. You did give me life, and I appreciate that." Tears came to his eyes and his chin quivered. "I always wanted to love you, but I was just too mad at you because you were not acting like I wanted you to." After more tears, he looked at me and said, "My, I feel relieved." He felt a real shift in his energy as he released his part of this relationship and allowed his mother to be responsible for her own selfishness and her inability to love.

He realized after he forgave her that she had never really had love to give to him or even to herself. Now that he had separated himself from the "deadlock" he'd been in with her—that of expecting something she could not give—he felt compassion for her. She had not had her own needs met as a child, and he had been demanding apples from an oak tree.

Maria

Alcoholism, smoking, drug addictions, and eating problems are often traceable to growing up in a family where basic needs are not met. Maria, an obese woman of twenty-eight, came for counseling. When Maria was young, her mother tried to make up for the love Maria did not get from her father, who was "too busy" at a new job. Instead of teaching her daughter in a positive, creative way how to get the love she needed from her father, the mother doubled her own nurturing efforts. A strong bond was formed between them.

Maria's mother identified with her daughter and "worried" about her. As Maria grew up, her mother had vocalized certain opinions of what Maria "should" be like and what she "should" do. Maria finished high school and went to college. She had little or no interest in men; she lived in the family home and never supported herself. She weighed about 225 pounds when she came to see me.

The first task was to assist her in being her own person. Maria took an apartment a distance from the family home. It was a shocking relief to her to learn that she could have thoughts of her own. She found she could make good decisions without aid from anyone. She became aware of her thought processes and began to observe herself and her reactions. Without any suggestions, she decided to lose weight. She put herself on an exercise program of walking and jogging daily. She discovered that she felt compelled to eat when she repressed her feelings, which she often did in order to appear "nice" and agreeable to family members. She decided not to repress her feelings and not to eat when she felt outer pressure, but rather to eat wisely when hungry.

Maria's basic work was to forgive herself for allowing others to take over and direct her life. She decided to be in charge of her body and her mind. She was proud of herself when she had lost twenty pounds by the end of six weeks, but equally proud that she had stood up for herself. She had listened quietly when her mother and other family members told her what she should do, then kindly told them that she would make up her own mind.

Did her mother really love her? Yes, she did love her—in a limiting way. Her mother loved her in a way that did not allow Maria to grow in her own self-awareness.

Every child needs love but no child thrives on "smother love." The fact that Maria could handle her situation kindly and gently indicates that many of her basic needs had been met by her parents. Some have to break out of prisons their parents have built for them. There is no easy way to do this, and it is necessary for the "prisoners" to see that they have allowed themselves to be imprisoned. They must forgive their captors for manipulating them and themselves for being manipulated.

Louise

At a conference I presented a workshop on unconditional love and forgiveness. I asked for a volunteer to demonstrate the process of forgiveness. Louise, a thin little lady of about seventy-five, offered her situation. She had a cousin of whom she had been most fond, but now she was finding herself uncomfortable in this cousin's presence. She had tried and tried, but found it impossible to forgive her cousin for voting a Democratic ticket in the last election.

As I looked into her dull, blue eyes, I saw no evidence of any love for her cousin or for herself. I was well aware that I had a real challenge—

with two hundred people present. I knew that I needed some love to start the process. I asked her to close her eyes and go back in her imagination to a time when she felt love for herself. She could not remember a time. Then I asked her to return to a time before age ten when she felt good about herself. She remembered when she was six years old she was given a new blue dress for Easter. I noticed a brightness in her face as she recalled the dress. I asked her how her hair looked at age six. She said she had long blond curls.

I asked her to close her eyes again. Then I asked the group to send their love out to little six-year-old Louise, with blond curls and beautiful blue eyes, wearing a new blue dress. We took several minutes sending love to her as we imagined this beautiful child of six. Louise began to relax, her skin began to glow, her lips (which had been thin and tight) began to soften. I asked her to take this love from the group into her heart and to allow it to flow throughout her whole body and feelings. This was a joyous moment for Louise.

Then I asked her to imagine her cousin in front of her. I asked her to tell her cousin how uncomfortable it had been to be out of harmony with her. She did this. Then I asked her if she was willing to cancel the expectation that her cousin would vote the way she, Louise, had voted. Louise was willing and did cancel the expectation. I asked her again to be aware of the love there in the group, and to send this love out to her cousin, regardless of how she voted.

Louise did this.

She smiled and said, "This sure feels good," as she put her hands on her chest. She was radiant with love and relief because she had forgiven her cousin. She looked warm and responsive.

When one who needs to forgive lacks love, hope and the willingness to restore a relationship—just as Louise had previously tried to forgive but nothing happened—a group can be most helpful. A group, large or small, can give support through its collective love, compassion, and understanding.

Pearl

Pearl was a woman in her early thirties who came to an introductory workshop on unconditional love and forgiveness. She had heard me say on a television show, "There is no situation that is unforgivable." At this workshop she sat and carefully absorbed every move that was made and every word I said. At the end, she came to me and said she had a need to forgive her father, but she was not sure it was possible. I invited her to come to a weekend workshop I would be leading in about a month. She had great concern about doing the forgiveness in a group setting. I assured her we could do it in a private session if she wished, but that the energy of the group often facilitates the process of forgiveness. It seemed to comfort her when I told her she would be able to feel the love and support of the group. At this workshop all the participants who registered were women, which made it easier for Pearl to share the intimate details of her relationship to her father.

As soon as there was an opportunity to do forgiveness work, Pearl volunteered. She said she had hated and feared her father most of her life, and therefore she did not believe her feelings could possibly change, but she was ready and willing to try anything because she could not go on with such fear and hate.

She had been doing some primal therapy where she screamed out her hate and rage, but she could not get past the anger, injustice, and fear she felt. Pearl said, "I think I need to go to a higher level." When she said this, I knew she was speaking from her own inner wisdom, and I also knew that truth: *a problem is never solved on the level where it is created; it has to be taken to a higher level to be solved or healed.*

Pearl shared with us that her father had molested her when she was three years old and continued this until she was eight. He threatened her life if she told anyone. She would be awakened out of a sound sleep at night by her father coming to her bed. At times, she feared going to sleep. She still had nightmares of terror. Even to the present time, she had experienced terror of the dark and had to sleep with a light on. As she became a teenager her father was still a threat to her because he seemed to take any liberty with her that occurred to him. She never knew what to expect.

"Pearl, how much longer do you want to carry

all this hate, fear, and anger, and all this hurt and pain which is your father's responsibility?" I asked.

"I want to give it up right now!"

(This is my way of involving the forgiver's will and of inspiring the person to take action.)

Reliving the agony of those incidents with her father was made easier with the support of those motherly, loving, compassionate women in the group. Pearl was able to tell her father what she would have preferred from him as her father. Then she was able to cancel all the expectations that he be a kind, loving, supportive, protective, nurturing father who would have wanted to put her welfare before his emotional and instinctual needs. She forgave him for all sexual acts of aggression toward her. Then she reached up in consciousness and thanked her Higher Self for protecting and caring for her, keeping her mind sane, and for loving her. She was then able to send love out to her father, just as he was, with all the problems during her childhood and at the present time. She breathed a great sigh of relief and said, "I feel lighter and free from a heavy load I've been carrying."

At the end of an hour and fifteen minutes, she was finally free of her hate and anger. She had compassion for her father who allowed his sickness to control him. At a later workshop Pearl forgave her mother for being a silent partner to her abuse. She felt her mother knew what was going on but was afraid to speak up and take a stand.

A short time after the forgiveness of her father, Pearl went to visit him. This visit was much different from others. This time she felt no terror or hatred, but only compassion and pity. She felt free and independent from him. Pearl has continued to work out the sexual problems caused by this abuse. She has a healthy outlook on life, and she can stand up for herself and take responsibilities that are hers to take.

Regardless of the offense, forgiveness of family members is possible. When we are willing to stop punishing ourselves for what others do and are willing to let go of the past, we can avail ourselves of love from the higher spiritual levels of our being. We can forgive all who have not met our expectations, demands, and conditions and once more return to our natural state of harmony and unconditional love.

THE LOCKHORNS

"HAS IT EVER OCCURRED TO YOU THAT IT MIGHT BE EASIER FOR YOU TO CHANGE YOUR EXPECTATIONS THAN FOR ME TO CHANGE MY HABITS?"

© 1986, courtesy of Bill Hoest and King Features.

Forgiving a Group or an Organization

Sometimes we feel out of harmony with a business, organization, agency, or a governmental body. When we feel we have been treated unfairly or dishonestly by a group or organization, it is most difficult to separate the offending individuals from the group itself. A conflict is set into motion, and we may become disenchanted with the whole organization, even when our dissatisfaction may be related to only one or two people in the group. Or, we may like the people, but disagree with the group's policies and practices.

Are we to forgive each offense or incident which each person has committed against us? If so, then how do we also deal with the organization as a whole? It sounds as complicated as opening a sewing basket and trying to unravel eight spools of thread that are all tangled up with each other.

In complex situations drama can help untangle feelings and sort out issues and characters. Psychodrama, instant theatre, and creative drama are useful tools to get to the depth of feelings. I also use gestalt techniques to sort out emotions and issues.

Forgiving a Nation

I was leading a workshop at a holistic health conference. A Japanese man in the group asked, "How can you forgive a whole organization?" I replied, "The best thing to do is to forgive all the individuals you know in the organization and be as specific as possible with what you are holding against them." I looked into his eyes and I knew I had not met this man's need even though I wanted to very much. I was aware of the other sixty-five people in the workshop whose specific questions I could and did answer.

Later, after giving a forgiveness demonstration, I directed the whole group in an exercise. At the end I asked those who were successful at experiencing forgiveness and relief to raise their hands. Nearly fifty did. Some had been able to forgive serious life-and-death situations. All the while I was aware that the Japanese man did not hold up his hand.

When the workshop was over, various people came to me to share their experiences. I wanted to speak with the Japanese man and felt relieved when I noticed he was not leaving. Soon the room was empty except for this man and his wife. As we walked toward each other, I felt I knew which organization he had referred to earlier. I held out my arms and said, "I represent the United States Government and its people. Please forgive us for all the injustices and suffering we have caused you and the Japanese people in the name of war." This man fell into my arms with his head on my chest and sobbed and sobbed like a child. As I tenderly held him, as I would a child, my mind raced back to 1942 when our two young daughters came home crying from little Toca's house, telling me that

Toca and her family had to leave their home and jobs and go away. I recalled my feelings of helplessness, and theirs, too, and how my heart had gone out to all the people in that predicament. My unconditional love flowed out to this man, his wife, and all who had been burdened with the injustice and pain of war.

He became conscious of himself, pulled back from me, and said, "Oh, pardon me!" He put his hands on his chest and lifted them up as he said, "I feel such a load lifted off my heart." His face was radiant and joyous. I shared my gratitude for the opportunity he gave me to unburden myself as well. We three held hands and looked into each other's tearful eyes with unconditional love and gratitude. Each time we made eye contact as the conference progressed, this man folded his hands together and gave me a "thank you" signal.

Forgiving a Congregation

In another group a young woman minister said she had recently been assigned to her first pastorate. Before she was sent to the congregation the church authorities had asked the local church board if they would accept a woman minister. The board members agreed that they saw no problem with that.

During the group work this minister brought up eight or ten expectations and demands the church people had put upon her which she could not fulfill. Each demand was related to her being a woman. She felt hostile and angry. I encouraged her to get her anger out, which she did through role playing. Then I took the simplest item on her list, hoping she could forgive it and then use the energy generated to forgive more complex situations. She could not forgive even the simplest incident.

This was years ago, before I was skilled in teaching people how to receive love from their Naphsha or how to shift consciousness to a higher level or how to use the love of the group. I knew that gratitude is one of the fastest ways of elevating consciousness, so I asked group members to say aloud what they were grateful for. I encouraged them to speak spontaneously, regardless of who else may be speaking, in order to make it work for everyone in the group. They named their health, friends, love, eyesight, beauty, sense of humor, hearing, family, children, and many other things. I could feel the energy of the group elevating.

Then I asked the minister, who had named many things for which she was grateful, if she was ready to forgive the people in her congregation. She said she was. Her consciousness had been elevated to the level of unconditional love through the gratitude exercise. We started with the simplest item on her list and then continued until her list was finished and she had forgiven each one involved.

At that time, and many times since, I have found gratitude to be a healing experience. Gratitude is a transpersonal energy which can heal our attitudes and elevate our consciousness. It was in this experience that I learned that one cannot heal a situation on the same level it was created. If we act in anger, or react angrily to something done to us (as in the minister's case), it cannot be forgiven while we are resentful or angry. Forgiveness can occur only on mental and spiritual levels—both levels are needed.

Forgiving Those Who Have Died

It is just as necessary to forgive people who have died as it is to forgive those who are living in their bodies. When we discover that we are still holding resentments towards someone, living or dead, it is important to forgive them immediately so we do not block love from the Naphsha.

If you discover you are still resenting someone who is deceased, that is good! Congratulate yourself for your awareness, for you now have the opportunity to forgive that person and free yourself of the negative attachment that keeps you blocked from love.

Sarah

Sarah came into my group saying, "I have done all my forgiveness."

"What do you mean, all your forgiveness?" I responded. She named a few relationships that needed forgiveness and said, "I'm all finished."

I suggested she let the all-wise part of her take

her back in memory into her childhood to see if there were any teachers, neighbors, or relatives that she needed to forgive. She was quiet for a moment.

"Oh, Mrs. O'Flannery! I had forgotten about her. Mrs. O'Flannery knew what everybody should do. She told my mother that she should stay home with us kids and not work. She used to get mad at us when we slid down the banisters. I still hate her! She was a trouble maker—nobody liked her!"

"Would you be willing to forgive Mrs. O'Flannery?"

"Oh, she's been dead for years," was the reply.

I pointed out that Mrs. O'Flannery had been very much alive in Sarah's mind all those years. When she realized that, she was able to forgive the old woman. After doing so, Sarah reported feeling very relieved. She had not realized how much resentment she was still carrying inside herself, and had not seen that, unless we forgive, resentments still remain intact even after the resented person dies.

Forgiving Ourselves

Some pray over things they have done
And make them seem like double.
Some straightaway forgive themselves
And save the Lord the trouble.

This is a quote from my good friend, the Reverend John Gaynor Banks, an Episcopal priest. He pointed out that many sensitive people have great difficulty coming to terms with errors they have committed. These sensitive people may be able to accept forgiveness for a while, but then they take the whole incident back upon themselves and start punishing themselves again.

How can we forgive ourselves? This can be answered on many levels and applied to many kinds of situations and circumstances. If we could truly see ourselves as we are, perhaps we would not have so much to forgive! The Sixth Attitude teaches us that those "without faults in their minds" shall see life as it is.

Often when we do things we view as wrong or "bad," we think *we* are wrong or bad, rather than that our actions at a given moment were in error. We tend to think *we* are our actions—if our actions have been unkind, we see ourselves as unkind.

Psychosynthesis distinguishes between one's self and one's behavior. The self has responsibility for the unkind act but the self is also capable of kind, thoughtful actions, for which it is also responsible. Sometimes we are blind to the good in ourselves. If we have a poor or distorted attitude towards ourselves, we cannot see ourselves objectively. Part of unconditional love is seeing the good in ourselves, as well as in others and in circumstances.

We all could stand to look at ourselves more clearly, without fault-finding. Most of us are more kind and forgiving to a stranger than we are to ourselves. When this is true, we have some work to do in regard to our self-image. We need to see ourselves in true perspective, to become aware that we can change our actions at will. We can appreciate the fact that the Naphsha, which is connected to the Source of life, gives us a view of who we really are!

We all have a lower unconscious which contains all our history and can guide us in designing our future. A higher unconscious contains our potential, the latent talents and abilities that lie beyond our expectations. There are techniques for bringing into conscious awareness the treasure from these unconscious "storehouses." These treasures enrich our lives by demonstrating that we are indeed unique and special!

As we've mentioned earlier, the word sin in Aramaic is an archery term which means "missing the mark; not achieving the goal expected." Sin is anything which holds us back from our potential, that which causes us to miss what is intended for us. When we have missed the mark we need to determine why, in order to make the needed adjustments and aim again. In our Western culture, missing the mark is considered terrible, or in some cases, irreparable—a splotch we must carry the rest of our lives. We go on existing, but not really living. We embroider the incident into our minds by going over it and over it, telling ourselves how terrible it was. Our guilt demands punishment, which may be in the form of:

1. Depriving ourselves of adventures or privileges we rightfully should have;

2. Depriving ourselves of relationships which could enhance our lives;

3. Depressing ourselves, getting into a "blue funk;"

4. Telling ourselves we have no right to live, and wishing to die; or

5. Developing a physical or emotional illness.

Sometimes we repress the memory of missing the mark rather than really dealing with it. This may not be the way we want to handle the problem, but we don't know what else to do; it helps us to survive. When we do this, we continue punishing ourselves unconsciously, or we project our "punisher" into our living environment: we blame "them out there" for punishing us and keeping us from what we desire. We go on through life, carrying this repression and thinking we don't hurt anyone (only ourselves!) until, perhaps, the doctor tells us we are suffering from some disease, or we can't figure out why we have no energy or enthusiasm for life.

The Second Attitude in the Essene *Code of Conduct* says that those conscious of their wrongs shall be cured of their mental stress. In the Aramaic language, mental, emotional, and physical are treated as one. Therefore, if we are conscious of our mistakes we will feel sorrow and regret, but we need to stay with those feelings only long enough to learn from them. Our next step is to allow the healing process to come to us from that elevated, transpersonal source, our Higher Self (Naphsha). It directs its healing energy through us when we hold ourselves open to love and forgiveness.

We do not have to stay in the punishing, lamenting attitude of, "I have committed a sin, and I have to grovel for months and years." The ancient Code teaches us to learn quickly from our experiences, to see our role in the situation, and to decide by the use of the will to get on with our lives. We can allow the healing from the Higher Self to ease our stress and restore us to perfect balance.

If we feel we have missed the mark, we may wish to say to the Source of life (the Creator, God, or whatever word you feel most comfortable with), "I have sinned against your law and against myself. I have missed the mark, and I regret this action. I am sorry for this mistake or wrong. I will to learn the lesson I need to learn from this experience. I will to go on with my life with greater wisdom. I now open myself to your healing, accepting love, allowing it to flow into me, releasing me from this stress I feel." Or you might wish to say, "Forgive me and let your love flow through me, cleansing and healing me from this missed opportunity."

Stop now and be silent for a few minutes and allow this to happen. Experience the silence as you breathe in this love from the Source. Then say, "I will begin now to live a new life. I totally accept your forgiveness." If you do not feel the love flowing from the Source, repeat the experience.

Use words that are meaningful and acceptable to you. Although the Source honors your sincerity and depth of feeling more than words, hearing the words aloud yourself is a very important part of this process. Hearing our own words is cleansing in itself. We do not have to stay in a problem—the Source always provides another chance. Can we be just as loving and benevolent with ourselves?

Now comes the official seal, the thanksgiving. Say, "Thank you, Source of life, for absolving my guilt, for the forgiveness, for the release, for the freedom from this missed opportunity. Thank you, I now allow this freedom from stress. Thank you for restoring my mind, my emotions, and my body, and for erasing the guilt I've been carrying."

Say aloud what you feel. Allow yourself to feel this gratitude and express it aloud in words. Years of pent-up tears may flow. Allow this. Whatever needs to happen, allow it to take place. Give yourself the freedom you need to experience this process. You deserve it.

Express in writing the details of your forgiveness experience. Write about the lessons learned, saving some space on the page to record additional thoughts, as insight continues to come, as you feel your gratitude deepen. Write also about the feelings of release, the freedom from tension.

Record the words you used to address the Source—this is important!

In the future, if you feel compelled to "take back" the incident and punish yourself again, read what you've written down. It will replenish you, free you from tension, renew your energy, and re-establish true perspective, which you deserve. Re-reading it at any time in the future may bring feelings of deep gratitude and renewed strength.

Forgiving Ourselves When We Were Children

I often talk to middle-aged or older people who are still punishing themselves for things they did when they were children. I ask them to look at themselves as a child or teenager as they would view a character in a movie. I ask them to observe the child or youth, to speak to him, and tell him just how they, as an adult, feel about those past events.

Usually these adults feel compassion and can easily love the child. They recognize that the child did the best he could under the circumstances. If they cannot feel loving and understanding, and are still caught up in the guilt and desire to punish, I use a psychosynthesis technique to raise consciousness to the place of the Higher Self (Naphsha) where there is understanding, compassion, forgiveness, and wisdom. From this transpersonal state, they can speak to the child with love and compassion and offer forgiveness. From the transpersonal level they also take the next step and tell themselves as adults how to get on with living.

Dora

At another conference, Dora wanted to be relieved of an overwhelming sense of guilt. The young woman said that when she was in junior high school in a multi-racial community, her very best friend, Susan, was black.

"We were inseparable from each other and loved each other as sisters. Then my family moved to another town and I attended an all-white school. I became aware of the prejudice, lack of openness, and lack of acceptance among my friends at this school. One day my former school's football team played my new school's team, and while I was with my friends, I saw Susan with her friends, and we came face to face. I became paralyzed! I opened my mouth to greet her and the words would not come out. My body became stiff and I could not move. A feeling of panic seized me. Neither of us spoke—Susan went on with her friends and I stood there, numb and helpless, like a stone. It was terrible!"

A silence fell over the group. Dora began to cry.

"I've been feeling so guilty all these years. I feel I have hurt Susan so deeply that she could never forgive me. I have so longed to know how she felt that day, but I have felt too guilty to try to find out."

At that moment I reached over to a young black woman namd Barbara sitting to my right and took her hand. I rose and said, "Dora, here is Susan. Tell her how you felt that day and how you have felt since," and I sat down.

The two young women stood facing each other as a hushed, loving silence in the group supported them both. Dora, with great agony, said, "I have been so miserable thinking of how I have hurt you. I have felt you could never understand what happened to me and would never forgive me."

Barbara, impersonating Susan, reached out and grasped Dora's shoulders and said, "I understood on that day. I knew you loved me as I loved you. I knew nothing could destroy that love for each of us. I did not speak up either because I did not want to cause any trouble."

The two hugged. Dora cried, as "Susan" held her.

"You forgive me, then?"

"Yeah, of course. There is nothing to forgive. Nothing can interfere with our love."

There were no dry eyes in the group as Dora told us the relief she felt and how her heart felt whole and warm again.

This incident is an example of "instant theater," where the whole group is aware of every word, gesture, and feeling of the one speaking. A feeling of unity pervades the entire group. Any member may play a needed role and may do so spontaneously without direction. This method can be effectively used in any kind of group setting.

An Exercise in Self-Forgiveness

Some of us feel more aligned and at home with the Higher Self (Naphsha) than with the Source (God). We look on the Higher Self as a more personal advocate, one who looks after our welfare, who knows our thoughts and desires, our weaknesses and strengths, our motives and intentions, and who is patient with us when we are immature and fail. We know the Higher Self to be a fair witness because it is all-loving, all-wise, forgiving, and patient.

One of the most effective self-forgiveness techniques is to reach up in consciousness to the Higher Self and ask forgiveness for specific actions and deeds. The following exercise can be used for present or past experiences.

You are going to ask Naphsha for forgiveness for some act you have performed or failed to perform, something you have felt guilty about. You will present to Naphsha each incident or act separately. Know and believe that Naphsha is eager to restore the flow of love to your consciousness and to your body, to re-establish the perfect connection that has been somewhat shut off by your feelings of guilt and shame.

You will contact Naphsha, above your head. Imagine it as a radiant light sending the energy of love and acceptance down to you. You will speak to Naphsha from your heart-felt feelings, saying what you would have preferred that you had done.

After you have confessed your regrets to

Naphsha, you will next identify with Naphsha because you *are* the Naphsha as well as the personal self who has confessed. As Naphsha, you will verbally forgive the personal self.

Then you will again speak from the personal self and thank Naphsha for forgiving you.

STEP 1: Sit in a comfortable chair or kneel, holding an attitude of openness. Reach up in consciousness to the Higher Self (Naphsha), which has watched over you all your life. Tell Naphsha what you feel at the moment. Take separately each incident needing forgiveness.

STEP 2: Stand with your eyes closed. Identify with Naphsha, that all-wise part of you. Identify with its qualities and feel compassion. Let this energy of compassion fill you. Identify with understanding, wisdom, and unconditional love. Take plenty of time to feel this. With your eyes still closed, look down upon the personal self, who may have acted unwisely or even foolishly and is asking for forgiveness. Speak to the personal self from that position of compassion, understanding, wisdom, and unconditional love, assuring the personal self of your forgiveness. From this wise and elevated place you can see the past clearly. You can see why and how everything happened as it did. Now in your great compassion as the Higher Self, send your unconditional love out in great abundance to the personal self, and cancel all conditions the personal self is holding against itself. Assure the personal self that no expectation, demand, or condition the personal self has put upon itself can separate your love from it. Continue sending unconditional love, assuring the personal self that it is *not* its actions, but is a personal self in the process of learning life's lessons. Surround it with peace of mind and comfort.

Now that you have completed STEP 1, asking for forgiveness, and STEP 2, identifying with the Higher Self and cancelling the self-imposed personal conditions, you are ready for STEP 3.

STEP 3: Take the position you assumed when you asked Naphsha for forgiveness, sitting on the chair or kneeling. Take time now to identify with the personal self that has just been forgiven. Feel how it feels to be forgiven, to have your slate clean. Feel your freedom. Feel the relief and goodness of what has just happened. With deep gratitude in your heart, thank Naphsha for the forgiveness you have just experienced. Let deep gratitude flood your whole being.

At this point you may wish to make a will statement, such as "I will to comfortably know that I am free of this past experience, and I will to remember how to avoid such circumstances in the future." In order to impress your new goal upon the unconscious mind, read or say aloud the will statement or the goal several times a day. While you are in this new state of just having been forgiven, the subjective mind is most easily impressed.

After you have successfully forgiven yourself you may find the opportunity to assist others in this process. Children and teenagers, as well as adults, carry heavy burdens of guilt because they have not learned this blessed process of unconditional love and forgiveness. Sharing with them on their level of awareness would be a loving act of service and humility.

Chapter 17

GOOD RUMORS

Human nature is loving, accepting, and forgiving. We were created to give and receive love. When we are giving and receiving love we are at our very best—physically, emotionally, mentally, and spiritually. We are functioning as we were created to function. We are in our natural state.

Khooba love is an attitude of unconditional positive regard, causing us to become aware of what is good in another or ourself or a situation. This love is a mind set (attitude) which includes the desire to express unconditional affection for others. It cues the brain to perceive the good in others—their fair and just actions, their wholesome desires and objectives.

A conversation with my daughter had caused me to consider the relationship between the attitude of love and the nurturing of others. My daughter, the mother of two children under age twelve, had told me that for a whole month after her children's birthdays they were unusually cooperative, even-tempered, kind, loving, full of energy, helpful, and a great joy to have in the home. She then told me that during the week of each of her children's birthdays the "birthday girl" had the privilege of making family decisions, with occasional assistance from the parents. These decisions included planning family entertainment activities such as picnics, visits to museums and movies; selecting menus for the evening meals; saying the blessing at the table; and making other choices. I realized that during this special birthday week these children felt loved and important. They were making a valued contribution to the family.

I began to think of my clients. Some of them had never experienced such a week, a day, or even an hour of this kind of recognition. I began to think about how most families seem to concentrate on the negative aspects of their children's behavior. According to natural law, whatever we cultivate, increases. Many of my clients' parents seemed to have actually cultivated "wrong" behavior in their children simply by holding the attitude that the children are wrong. I wondered how we can put khooba love to work in families, offices, businesses, or wherever people live or work together.

Jack

Jack was a professional golfer. One day he came in and announced that he would have to leave the country club where he worked and that he would have to find another job, which would undoubtedly mean he would leave the area. I inquired as to the ease of finding positions as a professional golfer and he told me that openings are rare. Although he seemed assured of his qualifications, he said openings were difficult to find.

"Why do you want to leave this job?" I asked.

"I can't stand it any longer!" he fired back. "I've had it!" Evelyn, the owner, inherited the country club from her father when he died. She doesn't know anything about golf! Absolutely nothing about running a club."

I noticed how much emotion he had when he mentioned Evelyn, and I said, "Tell me about Evelyn."

"She knows nothing about a business, let alone golf!"

He went on to say that they were getting ready for a big tournament and he had told Evelyn they needed to order twenty-four golf carts.

"Yesterday, I asked why the carts had not arrived, and she said, 'Oh, they came this morning when you were at the barber shop. When I saw the bill, I just told them to load them up and take them back.' I just saw red when she said that! Then I told her that we would have to cancel the tournament because we can't have a tournament without carts. She told me to call the golf equipment dealer and have them bring the carts again. When I called, they yelled at me, 'What kind of an outfit are you, anyway? You had us deliver them, then reload them and bring them back and unload them, and now you want them! Make up your mind!' I was so embarrassed I made up my mind right then: I'm leaving!"

I looked at Jack sitting on the edge of his chair, his face flushed.

"Does Evelyn do anything well?"

"Yes, she runs the banquet room in great style when we have tournaments. She serves excellent food, and it is served beautifully. She makes everyone feel at home and comfortable. She is great at that."

"Is there a good place to start rumors at the club?"

"Yes, the coffee shop."

"Are you willing to work at making that a great place to work?" I queried.

He told me firmly that he was. I then asked him to go to the coffee shop that afternoon and tell one or two people what a good job Evelyn does in the banquet room when you have tournaments. I told him, "You have to be honest—don't say anything that isn't true." I asked him to start another good rumor the next day, and to do this for five days, but to be sure to do it very naturally and quietly.

The next week Jack *waltzed* into my office. He was smiling and looked very happy.

"Guess what?" he beamed, "I'm not moving! Last week when I saw you, Evelyn and I were not even speaking but I guess those rumors got around to her. She came to me yesterday and told me how happy she was that I was doing such a good job with the tournaments and the golf shop. And then she smiled and said, 'Jack, I'm going to stick to the banquet room, and I want you to run all the golfing business.'"

Jack was able to give his khooba love, to see what was fair, what was good and wholesome in Evelyn. He was willing to put this love out into his environment. He did not stop with Evelyn; he continued spreading good rumors about other people at the club. They began to ask him what caused him to change from the way he used to be, and he told them about unconditional love.

About three months later he had a birthday, and when he went to work the morning of his birthday, there was a long paper banner across the entire front of the clubhouse reading, "We love you, Jack."

You are invited to go out and start good rumors! Good rumors thrive in families, offices, shops, and restaurants. When you start looking for the good, there seems to be no limit to what you can discover.

I once suggested to some parents that they start a good rumor about their teenage son. They had been having difficulty communicating with him, and I wondered how long it had been since the boy had heard his parents mention any of his positive qualities. I asked them what good things they could say about their son. Silence! After a while they still could think of nothing to say about him.

"Well," I said, "he's breathing, isn't he? Think of what you would do if he stopped breathing? You can start a good rumor about his good health, his appetite, his ability to sleep—you can start a good rumor about anything positive. You may have to go back a few years and start a good rumor about what he did or what others thought of him when he was a little boy. Start anywhere, but *start!*"

I used to tell my grandchildren what I enjoyed and appreciated about them when they were small and just learning to walk and talk. One day a five-year-old granddaughter pulled her little chair up in front of me and said, "Tell me when I was little, Grammy." She never tired of seeing my face glow with love and wonder as I recalled the cute and clever things she said and did when she was a toddler.

My good friend Vivian Markham shared a "recipe" for seeing the good in others, and I have shared it with many parents who have found it very effective. Vivian and her family returned from Africa, where her husband had been a missionary doctor, when their children were fifteen, thirteen, and twelve years old. The children had become so oriented to the African lifestyle that they suffered culture shock upon returning to the United States. Vivian was concerned particularly about her son and his inability to relate to boys and girls his own age.

She took a manila folder and began to cut out magazine pictures of boys his age relating to others. This gave her a positive visual image of how it could be—how her son could find ways of relating and making friends and becoming productive in his school relationships. Her son began to make friends at school and develop socially.

These folders are not to be shared or shown to the child, but are solely for the parent who needs to know and believe that the child can develop normally and naturally. One mother was so proud of her folder that she exuberantly showed it to her child and it had a negative effect on the child.

Starting good rumors in the workplace is beneficial, especially if you are having difficulty relating to a particular person—often referred to as "the one person at work I can't stand." Usually this person is not practicing khooba love, but is instead concentrating on negative qualities. It is up to you to spread good rumors to counter negative attitudes and feelings.

Use good rumors at home. You can refer to a relative's latent potentials as well as to observed behaviors. For example, if you are trying to figure out how to put something together or take it apart, you can call the person you are concerned about to assist you since "he has such good ideas about mechanical things." Refer to natural abilities, giving credit for past efforts or experiences you have appreciated. Later you can tell other family members about this person's abilities or the help that was given. You can give this loved one the opportunity to help, or can ask his opinion on something, such as, "I was wondering what other young people feel about. . . ." The important thing is that you're giving credit and recognition.

When we are unhappy or out of harmony in our environment, we unconsciously start framing goals to get us out of the uncomfortable situation. At work, for instance, we may unconsciously set up a situation resulting in our being fired. This kind of circumstance can also occur in a marriage or other relationship where we are unhappy.

One of the foreign students at our training center could not qualify for a student visa because she was not a full-time student. She could not legally get a job in this country because she had only a visitor's visa. The only job she could legally obtain was with her own government, so she worked at her country's consulate in Los Angeles. Her job was very important to her because of her financial situation. One day she came into my office and said, "I have just discovered how I have been setting myself up to get fired." She told me how intensely she disliked the people with whom she worked—especially her boss—and that she was beginning to realize how she had gradually withdrawn from her fellow workers, immersing herself in her work. When her boss called her into his office one day, she asked if he wanted her to do more work. He replied, "No, I only want you to be more open and responsive to the other people in the office."

I asked her what was good about her boss. She named several things. I asked if she was willing to start a good rumor. She said she was, and we discussed how she could do this. She came the next week with a fine report. Then we discussed how she could start good rumors about the other people in the office. It is amazing how fast this works! In three weeks she was enjoying her job and the people in the office.

Think about where you can start good rumors. Look at your life and see what is good about it. Use khooba love to make your life joyous and pleasurable.

Rules for Starting a Good Rumor

1. Decide that you want to change the atmosphere in your workplace, home, or other environment.

2. Decide that you will put some effort into creating this change. Decide to do this as your personal project. Tell no one what you are doing (then you won't have to explain anything to anyone).

3. Make a list of the positive qualities about another person and keep it to yourself. You will see and hear plenty of negative qualities. You do not deny the negatives, but you choose not to focus on them for the time being, in order to concentrate on the positive qualities.

4. Once you have the list of things you like, admire, and appreciate about this person, select one item with which to start the first rumor. At lunch, on a coffee break, or whenever appropriate, say to a fellow worker, family member, or whomever, something like, "I really admire how neat and clean Nancy always looks." Or, "I appreciate John's always being so prompt." This must be a true feeling. If the response is negative, don't comment—just let it be. Even though you may agree, you are looking for and have found the good, so concentrate solely on it. You may repeat the good rumor if you wish.

5. In a day or so, select another quality you admire and share this with another person. Continue this process, and you'll soon see the atmosphere change and relationships improve.

Chapter 18

PRAYER AND MEDITATION

In the last century human beings have become powerful in mastering the laws of nature. We have discovered laws that supersede other laws. We have gone to the Moon, circled Earth and other planets, plumbed the depths of the oceans, built skyscrapers, created computers and machines that talk and act. Yet so many of us know very little about our inner nature, the laws that rule the unconscious world.

Although the technological power we have harnessed is awesome, it is not all constructive. With the flip of a switch we can set in motion the destruction of all our billions of brothers and sisters and make our earth uninhabitable for centuries. I believe this potential for destruction which we ourselves have created is the result of our having developed outer power without balancing it with inner power. The majority of us have not been in touch with the essence of our being, our soul, our Naphsha, our Higher Self. Having developed our brain and not our heart, we find ourselves out of balance, and we suffer for it.

In his book, *The Act of Will,* Roberto Assagioli stated, "The remedy for these evils—the narrowing and eventual closing of the fatal gap between Man's external and internal powers—has been and should be sought in two directions: *the simplification of his outer life and the developing of his inner powers.*"[1] Those who are gravely concerned for the present human condition might suggest returning to nature and living the simple life. But we cannot all abdicate our responsibilities and leave our posts, although we may at times feel a great urge to do so. Assagioli said, "The evil does not lie in the technological powers themselves but in the *uses* to which we put them and in the fact that Man has allowed them to overwhelm and enslave him."[2]

Resistance to the prevailing negative trends in modern life calls for much determination, firmness, persistence, clearsightedness, and wisdom. Those are the qualities of inner power available to each of us if we are aware of our purpose and intention. However, with the pressures of time and activities feeding our outer life, we can lose sight of that inner purpose. Assagioli told us:

Fundamental among these inner powers, and the one to which priority should be given, is the tremendous, unrealized potency of man's own *will*. Its training and use constitute the foundation of all endeavors. There are two reasons for this: the first is the will's central position in man's personality and its intimate connection with the core of his being—his very self. The second lies in the will's function in deciding what is to be done, in applying all the necessary means for its realization and in persisting in the task in the face of all obstacles and difficulties.[3]

The self decides by use of its will what the self will do, will allow, and will permit. We, you and I, decide what our lives will be like; we make that choice daily. However, because so many choices are unconscious, we usually are unaware that they govern our lives.

The Essenes, two thousand years ago, chose what kind of life they would have, and they clearly knew how to make choices to support that life. They chose to live in peace and be peace servers. They had definite attitudes to assume and maintain to that end.

Prayer: Communication with the Source

Individuals and groups of people have prayed since the beginning of history. Prayer—communication with the divine within us and beyond us—is a basic human instinct. In times of need we respond to this instinct, reaching out for something greater than our self, for guidance, strength, help, and insight. To the extent that we have faith and trust, that we give of ourselves and remain open to answers, they will come.

Prayer is largely an appeal of the heart; it stems from feeling and desire. It may also involve physical and mental processes. It is a petition, intercession, or thanksgiving. It is more than asking; it is a lifting up and calling down from the Source.

In *The Silent Path,* Michal J. Eastcott reminds us of Christ's words, "Ask and it will be given you, seek and ye shall find; knock and it shall be opened unto you." He says these words from the

Gospel of Saint Luke frame a fundamental existential law—the law of demand and supply. When a need makes itself known, it evokes a response from the universal supply. Vacuums are filled. Efforts set in motion bring about corresponding returns. When our heart, mind, and will are aligned with universal laws, needs are supplied— often in miraculous ways. The runner with a crushed leg holds in mind how he will run again: his prayers help him become a champion. The refugee family with grateful hearts and the willingness to work hard become productive and successful members of their community.

The riches of life are available. We need to link ourselves with the supply. We must faithfully present our needs, knowing they will be met if our hearts are dedicated to serve.

Eastcott says:

> Framing a demand, be it physical, emotional or mental, or all three, creates an evocative current; it acts with pulling power magnetically attracting that to which it is keyed. A channel is created by the focus, a magnetism is exerted by the need; according to the level on which the appeal is made, so will be the quality of the response. Like attracts like, presenting a similar vibration which offers thus a channel for that which is sought.[4]

Prayer is the cry of the heart that recognizes forces greater than itself, forces to reach out to, to call upon to fulfill a need. Through prayer and meditation we can be the recipients of the goodness of life.

Prayer can help us maintain attitudes and goals. It can help us achieve material goals simply because it creates a harmony within itself, aligning us with the Source of life. All goals in harmony with that Source are easily attained. During the Korean War approximately one-third of those imprisoned by the North Koreans proved resistant to brainwashing. United States authorities tested and analyzed these men to determine the common factor among them. The only common personality trait, experience, or habit displayed—regardless of the prisoner's race, creed, or national heritage—was the use of prayer. The Turkish prisoners, all Moslems, proved to be one hundred percent resistant to brainwashing, whereas only thrity-three percent of the British, Australian, and American prisoners resisted.[5] Moslem prayer, performed ritually three times a day, involves the total individual on a physical, emotional, mental, and spiritual level. The Moslems aligned themselves completely with their Source, and there was no space for the brainwashing to take hold. They knew who they were; no one could confuse them.

Meditation:
Living in Harmony with the Source

Meditation is a mental process that involves the heart, soul, and will. Thought is an energy unseen, but dynamic. It is a real power. Through meditation, one may use thought to build, feed, and maintain an idea or image. Meditation is an inner mental action, a deliberate use of thought to fulfill a specific purpose. It is a redemptive process. This process acts on deep levels of our being, giving us a quality that can cause major positive transformations to occur within our lives.

Creative imagination and visualization are important factors in meditation. By learning to control and direct the imagination, we become its master and can use it to create harmony, beauty, and joy. Concentration is one of the first steps in meditation. Through the use of "seed thoughts" we learn control of the mental process, allowing us to form thoughts at will. Since meditation uses thought forms, imagination, and visualization—all productive tools— we have a *grave responsibility to use this power only for the good of all humanity.*

Scientific research has allowed us to validate the subjectively experienced benefits and value of meditation:

> Among major changes which occur during meditation are a slowing of breath and heart rate, decrease in oxygen consumption, lowering or stabilization of blood pressure, and decrease in skin conductivity. Additionally, the EEG (electroencephalogram, or recording of electric currents in the brain) shows characteristic patterns of change during meditation. It is important to note that this brain-wave pattern

during meditation is not the same as that during sleep. The pattern of response to external stimuli is similar to that of a person during a waking state, since meditation is not accompanied by drowsiness when practiced properly.[6]

Lawrence LaShan, a pioneer in therapeutic and ethical implications of meditation, explains why we are willing to discipline ourselves to meditate:

> We meditate to find, to recover, to come back to something of ourselves we once dimly and unknowingly had and have lost without knowing what it was or where or when we lost it. We may call it access to more of our human potential or being closer to ourselves and to reality, or to more of our capacity for love and zest and enthusiasm, or our knowledge that we are a part of the universe and can never be alienated or separated from it, or our ability to see and function in reality more effectively. As we work at meditation, we find that each of these statements of the goal has the same meaning. It is this loss, whose recovery we search for, that led the psychologist Max Wertheimer to define an adult as "a deteriorated child." It is our fullest "humanhood," the fullest use of what it means to be human, that is the goal of meditation. Meditation is a tough-minded, hard discipline to help us move towards this goal.[7]

Types of Meditation

There are many different types of meditation.

Various types serve different needs. Just as an exercise program should be carefully suited to our physical needs, meditation should be suited to our spiritual needs. As these needs change we should be able to change the style of our meditation.

I did some psychosynthesis guide work with a young man who had been impotent for five or six years and who had not had normal sexual relations in that time. He did not sleep well at night, was nervous, and needed much rest. His wife, a stout, matronly young woman, had assumed all the family duties with the children and the household. She was concerned that her husband was quickly becoming the center of family attention. She said, "I don't want the family to make him an invalid by all this attention and tiptoeing to keep things quiet in the house; the children need to be active."

In two individual sessions with this man, I saw clearly that in his striving to be a "spiritual person" he had disregarded his physical life. I designed a meditation which gave energy to his whole life—physical, emotional, mental, and spiritual. In a few months he wrote a joyous letter, with special greetings from his wife, saying that their relationship was normal and active again. He had more energy and was sleeping well, and the whole family was relating better. Three years later he had a demanding job and an avocation that required much of him. He was well and able to cope with all this responsibility. His wife was fifteen pounds lighter, looked younger, and was happy in her new job. The children were active and harmonious.

Meditation has been an integral part of psychosynthesis since its inception. Assagioli was well aware of the effectiveness of meditation in changing life patterns, whether psychological, physical, or situational. Psychosynthesis utilizes three basic types of meditation: reflective, receptive, and creative. As you become familiar with the practice of meditation, you will be able to select the type that best suits your needs.

You may wish to use reflective meditation to gain an objective, holistic view of circumstances in your life, to be able to see what may be needed or eliminated. Receptive meditation is a way for you to receive guidance, direction, ideas, and information from higher sources than your own mind and personality. Creative meditation may be used when you wish to create new goals, concepts, ideas, and projects.

Reflective Meditation

Reflective meditation uses the mind like a mirror—allowing thoughts and ideas to reflect upon its surface, bringing insight and knowledge. The will, a most important element of meditation, can hold the mind steady so the reflection is clear and concise. Learning to hold the mind steady and focused on the desired subject may require practice and concentration. When you have mastered this ability to hold the mind steady, to perceive the subject you wish to pursue, you are ready for reflective meditation. The process begins by selecting an interest or an idea upon which to concentrate.

A businessperson may reflect upon his business, attempting to clarify distressing elements. He may reflect upon qualities he needs, such as courage or patience, to make the business succeed. Another may wish to use reflective meditation for the purpose of self-development. He might concentrate on some universal qualities—unconditional love or wholeness (especially if healing is needed), beauty, or any of the psychological or spiritual qualities desired.

Assagioli states:

> The most important, indeed, the most indispensable, subject for meditation in achieving personal psychosynthesis is reflective meditation on one's self. By means of it one is able to distinguish between pure self-consciousness or awareness of the Self and the psychological elements or parts of one's personality at various levels.[8]

Receptive Meditation

A clear understanding of the difference between reflective and receptive meditation can be gained by regarding the mind as an "inner eye." In reflective meditation the mind's eye is directed horizontally. It observes the object, the theme of the meditation, the seed thought, or the various aspects of the personality. In receptive meditation the mind's eye is turned upwards, seeking to discover insight at a higher level than that of ordinary consciousness.

The first stage is *silence.* To receive an intuition, an inspiration, a message, or a stimulus to action from the superconscious or transpersonal level of our being, we must eliminate whatever might impede its descent into our consciousness. This is why silence is necessary. One person accustomed to meditating reported the following experience:

> I was immersed in a profound meditation and knew that I had reached a limpid, radiant state, when this thought crossed my mind: "I know I am at this level, and yet I am deaf and blind and can hear and see nothing." A moment passed and then this humorous reply came: "If you were silent as well, you would be able to see and hear!"

Receptive meditation may prove somewhat difficult if you have an overly developed concrete, thinking mind. The objective mind is not easily stilled. Nevertheless, silence alone permits the higher, abstract mind to bring its message into the lower mind. This alignment is required in order for receptive meditation to be effective. The concrete mind usually wants to objectify, to analyze, to react. This part of the mind has been trained over the years to name, to see relationships, and to analyze. Now its task is altogether different—to be still, silent, and simply to observe without categorizing.

Initially this task may generate a resistance to

the whole idea of receptive meditation, which manifests itself by a feeling of sluggishness. Assagioli cautions us about this reaction:

> In other cases the opposite difficulty arises: a sense of heaviness or somnolence comes on. This is to be strenuously resisted, since it may lead to a state of passivity in which elements erupt from the unconscious, particularly from the lower and collective unconscious, or from the extraneous psychic energies. As soon as one is aware of this happening, the condition must be interrupted and the meditation suspended, at least for a while. In general, receptive meditation presents greater difficulties than reflective meditation, and its practice must be vigilantly conducted if damaging effects are to be avoided.[9]

These frequent reactions—becoming overly active or overly passive to the point of drowsiness—render receptive meditation impossible. These reactions must be dealt with before proceeding. If this happens, you need to take a little extra time and effort to train the mind to be open, still, alert, and receptive. Bring your innate power of the will into the process! Use the energy of the will to direct the lower, concrete mind into a waiting, observing, and alert position. At the same time use the will to direct attention upward towards the transpersonal realm, into the intuitional levels of the Higher Self, to receive ideas and messages.

Inner contact. This form of receptivity can be

called contact because it is almost like the physical sense of touch. It puts us in contact with the energy of the Higher Self or Naphsha. We become receptive to its influences and aware of its quality and nature. We can then gradually identify or unify ourselves in consciousness—however partially and momentarily—with that spiritual reality or being.

> By this inner nearness, by this "touch" of the Higher Self, we are harmonized, vivified, recharged with energy; or with that which we specifically need at the time, and which the Self is trying to convey to us. Its effects are clarifying and enlightening; we are filled with certainty, courage, joy; we feel renewed and ready to go back to the arena of personal life and meet its emergencies and challenges. We feel that some higher power has descended upon us and added a greater power to our own. Repeated contact can lead to a certain degree of blending or infusion by the Higher Self or the radiation from superconscious levels. When this pervasion becomes to some extent permanent, it is termed being a "self-infused personality."[10]

Sometimes we are energized after an inner contact; we may have an urge to act upon something we have been considering or upon an entirely new idea. Meditation Group for the New Age offers some suggestions on this aspect of meditation:

> We may receive impressions from the Self . . .

through an urge to action. We become aware of it as a definite urge to do something, to undertake a task or duty in some field of service, or sometimes it may be an urge toward inner action of some sort, to the changing of something in ourselves. This type of impression is what the Quakers—who have practiced this art of receptive meditation and silence more than others in the West—call "concern."

Again, we need to discriminate carefully between urges coming from the Self or some high, superconscious level, and those coming from the middle or lower unconscious. The way in which they appear in the consciousness is similar, but a difference will be found in the *quality* and *content* of the urge. Whenever it takes the form of a call to a great mission or to some action of personal advantage, we should regard it with suspicion. An urge of this type is normally of lower origin and is spurious and should, of course, be dismissed.

Registration. To register what happens in the meditation is a most important step in our growth process. Often the ideas or experiences are so vivid and alive that we "just know" we will always remember them. We cannot always assume this "knowing" will stay with us. As we move from this experience to emphasize another aspect of our personality, such as thinking or feeling, the meditation experience is likely to become less vivid. Meditation Group for the New Age offers some suggestions on registration:

Every impression, whatever its type or the way in which it is received, should be accurately and immediately registered in writing. As mentioned previously in connection with reflective meditation, the higher impressions are often vivid and clear at the moment of reception, but they have a curious tendency to disappear rapidly from the field of consciousness and if not caught and registered at once they are apt to be lost. Also, the very fact of formulating them and writing them down helps us to understand them better; sometimes during writing the impression will develop, and we will continue to receive it. Writing can, in fact, be used as a technique for evoking inspiration; it creates a convenient channel for the higher impressions. But while writing one should always remain alert and fully aware, not permitting any form of "automatic" writing, which can easily have undesirable and even dangerous effects.

Another interesting aspect of receptivity is the *delayed reception of impression.* It often seems that nothing happens during receptive meditation; we remain in a state of blankness and do not become aware of anything new except, perhaps, a sense of quiet, rest, and refreshment. But this does not necessarily mean that the meditation has been useless and unsuccessful, for quite frequently some impression or inspiration will come into our consciousness later in the day, or even another day. It may be in another meditation or at some time when we are engaged in quite different activities; it may be in some moment of relaxation or on waking in the morning, but whenever it is we will recognize a connection between the apparently unsuccessful meditation and the subsequent inspiration. This connection will be evident when the answer which we sought to some question or problem flashes into our minds, but there can also be a less dramatic but equally true delayed reception of impression to which we should be alert.

Therefore, after meditation, we should always keep an inner attitude of watchfulness and attentiveness—what is called when developed, a "meditative attitude"—during the whole day.

Creative Meditation

As the name implies, creative meditation is one in which we create. For example we could use creative meditation to visualize a fulfilling relationship. We could create in our meditation a wholesome atmosphere in our workplace, or create the kind of job that would draw upon our talents and abilities and be worthy of us. In creative meditation we always create the solution to problems. We see, hear, and feel the fulfillment of what it is we want and what would be good for us and others. Meditating is like baking a cake—after we learn the basic rules, we can create many different kinds of cakes.

Assagioli wrote:

Meditation can be creative because it is "inner

action." A contrast is sometimes made between meditation and action, but this is erroneous. The mastery and application of psychological and spiritual energies *are* actions, for they require will, training, and the development of appropriate techniques; and above all because they are effective—they produce results.[11]

Motives and goals. In creative meditation we need to examine our motives and clarify our goals. When we meditate we are manipulating energy, creating change; this makes it all the more important that we be aware of our objectives and of their consequences. Here are two examples of looking at motives and clarifying goals.

Participants in the Meditation Research program I conducted from 1965 to 1968 were required to select a project in which they were to use creative meditation. One participant presented her project for approval, which was to create a great sum of money through her business. Her goal was to provide this money for her teenage son so he would not have to work in his young adulthood—then he would love her more. This participant did not have the foresight and awareness to realize that her project, if successful, might actually interfere with her son's normal development. By not working he might miss opportunities for growth. Her motive to have her son love her more might not in any way be related to him not working as a young adult. We have no right to try to affect others in our meditation, unless, of course, we have been invited to do so and it is for the good of all concerned. We have enough work to do on ourselves to last us a lifetime, without seeking to work on others!

As another participant in the Meditation Research program contemplated her project, she decided for the next three years "to be a loving person." She aimed to expand her consciousness, to develop her capacity to love, and to be a more open and giving person. This young woman, a teacher, used creative meditation principles each day. She visualized herself as a loving, understanding, gentle teacher, and sent the energy of love out to her pupils. She felt love in her body, in her emotions, and in her thoughts. She held the attitude of unconditional love throughout the school day as much as possible.

Even though this teacher never told anyone about her project, her principal began to refer the disturbed, unhappy children to her. At first she thought this was unfair. Then she said to herself, "This will be a great test for me. I will have a greater opportunity to really practice my project." At the end of three years this teacher was a happy, joyous, loving person. She was open and giving. She had not tried to change anyone. However, thirty-plus children in her classroom each year learned what it is like to have a loving teacher.

As we clarify our motives and decide our purpose, we hold the attitude of goodwill towards ourselves and others. We are now ready to start a program in creative meditation. We want to make changes in our lives—perhaps to change some habits in our thinking or acting. We may have a goal to have good health, for example. Perhaps we carry around a few too many pounds. Although we have thought about exercising, it usually doesn't get beyond a fleeting mental process. Now we will use our will to decide what we want, and what we need to do to bring our goal to fruition. If the goal is to exercise, we make a plan, enlist the will to carry out the plan, and reap the results. We can create a meditation that will help us to this end.

We use our creative power of thought all the time. We can learn to use this innate power to create what we need and want, or let it randomly create what we don't want. In *Your Mind is Your Destiny,* Dr. William Parker states:

The brain is the vehicle of mind, and its workings are awesome. When we speak of mind, we are dealing with law. We were fashioned and evolved in a law-abiding universe, and are sustained and maintained by both physical and spiritual laws which work. The law of mind normally does not work as quickly, for example, as the law of gravity. Spiritual laws, however, supersede the physical. This is why *a thought can become a thing.*

Abuse of the physical laws can be overcome by moving to the spiritual level. Using mind, through the brain, we can recondition the body, for the spiritual is not only the higher level, it is, in essence, all.

The thoughts we hold must materialize in some way. They limit us or set us free. Our beliefs about life, about ourselves, about our destinies are the keys to what we experience and what unfolds for us.

You do have a choice. Use your mind to conceive that which is beautiful, perfect, whole. The law is: so within, so without. [12]

Prayer and meditation are natural tools. We are not dependent upon anyone for their use. They have the power to change life for the better. They are free, and they are available twenty-four hours a day.

Preparation for Meditation

Effective meditation requires adequate preparation. Part of the preparation is the decision to meditate. It is a decision to commit to a program which requires time, study, and discipline— little benefit is derived from occasional meditation. We discover the real value of a meditation program when it becomes a total commitment to a way of life. Our energy, goals, and attitudes are directed towards this way of life. We could say it is a life stance. It is a willingness to take responsibility for our life, and to create a wholesome healing atmosphere for ourselves and others.

After deciding to begin a program of meditation we must plan a time for it. Some type of consciousness-raising study, such as reading an inspirational book, prior to the actual meditation is most helpful. It expands our awareness and prepares our receptivity.

Training the body to relax for meditation is essential. It releases energy and promotes general health. Sit on a chair with your spine as straight as is comfortable. Feet should be flat on the floor; hands on the thighs or palms down in the lap. You may choose to sit on the floor or on a mat in the lotus position, with your feet folded in front of you, and hands comfortably resting on your knees or thighs. Keep your head erect, but not stiff, so that if your eyes were open, you'd be naturally gazing straight ahead. *Never lie down to meditate!*

Thoroughly relax the physical body. Eliminate all concerns and tensions. Scan the body, making note of any tension, then adjust the body to promote serenity and relaxation. Allow your breathing to be natural and normal. Become aware that life is breathing you. You can alter your breath, but you cannot stop breathing. Let life breathe you, establishing a natural rhythm.

Calm the emotions. If there is an emotional disturbance or concern, put it aside until the meditation is completed. This is not suppression, but suspension. We actually need to train our emotional responses to wait their turn when necessary. However, it is important to give full attention to the particular concern after the meditation.

Still the concrete aspect of the mind. Focus the center of consciousness inward, in an observing manner. The mind is an instrument, an inner tool from which we dis-identify if we are to make use of the will. We cannot really control the mind while we are wholly identified with it. We need a certain "psychological distance" or detachment in order to see the mind as a tool that belongs to the self but is not the self.

Outline For Meditation

1. PREPARATION
   Close your eyes.
   Relax the physical body; be aware of your breathing.
   Feel gratitude that life is breathing you and causing your heart to beat.
   Calm the emotions.
   Still the mind.

2. REFLECTIVE STAGE
   Raise your consciousness upward to the Higher Self.
   Choose a quality of the Higher Self, such as serenity, compassion, patience, peace, courage, or joy.
   Concentrate on this quality for two or three minutes, seeing this quality being expressed in your life or in the world.

3. RECEPTIVE STAGE
   Discontinue the reflective thoughts.
   Reaching toward the Higher Self, *hold* the

thoughts or ideas that came in stage 2 in the light of the Higher Self.

Imagine the seed thought or idea like a vessel to be filled with the light of the Higher Self. This stage should last only a minute or so.

4. CREATIVE STAGE

With the seed thoughts and ideas you received in stages 2 and 3, and from the quality of the Higher Self you chose, see the forms of that quality as a creative force.

Imagine this force changing our world in situations or changing something in your life that you want to change.

Using visualization and your creative imagination, create positive, active pictures.

Do this for several minutes.

Say: "May ————*(the quality)*———— be the keynote of my life. May I truly express this quality."

5. CLOSING

Let all the images go.

Become aware of your breathing and your body; become aware of where you are sitting and of the room where you are.

Open your eyes when you feel ready.

In the beginning the meditations should not last more than ten or fifteen minutes. If you should become over-stimulated during or after meditating, discontinue the meditations for a day or so. Then when you begin again, meditate for a shorter period of time.

CONCLUSION
A *Summary of Unconditional Love and Forgiveness*

When we have a need to forgive, we have usually come to an impasse in a relationship with ourselves or another. If we look closely we will discover that we were expecting or demanding something we did not get. The demands which were not met represent the way we feel it should be or should not have been. If we then withdraw our love—refusing to give love until the conditions are met—we are practicing "conditional love."

Forgiveness can take place only within ourselves, since we are the ones whose expectations, demands, or conditions are not being met. To forgive means to cancel. What needs to be cancelled? The mental or emotional demands which we have decided must be honored in order for us to give love. The wrong of another cannot be cancelled. Cancelling is not a pardon that wipes out or restores the wrong of another. An act cannot be changed—it is a past event, a record of what happened. Cancelling is neither forgetting nor the inability to remember a wrong committed. This would be impractical, as we need to remember the situation in order to protect ourselves in the future. However, we do not remember the act to use it against another; we remember it only to learn from it.

Cancelling involves making a conscious shift from the emotional level (our feelings about the wrong done) to the mental level (how we would have preferred it had been). We state what we would have preferred. Having done this, we are able to shift further to the transpersonal or spiritual level and allow the love from our Naphsha to flow into us again. We begin to look at the positive and away from the negative. Changing our focus enables us to see the good in self, in others, and in situations—and to let go of the impasse or conflict.

The conflict, then, is between what we perceive (the way we see that it happened) and what we prefer. This conflict blocks the flow of love from our Higher Self (Naphsha). It's as though we're trying to water the garden while standing on the hose! We are not aware that we are on the hose unless we're aware that the flow is blocked.

When we block the flow of love, it's as though we're trying to water the garden while standing on the hose!

Any time we are not feeling love from the Source of life, or we are not feeling love for others and ourself, it's time to get off the hose and allow love to flow.

We are the only one who can remove the block. How do we do it? By becoming aware of the good in others, in ourself, and in situations; and by becoming aware of—and feeling gratitude for—the universal love expressed in every living thing. This is guaranteed to cause love to begin to flow into us once again! We all have the power to choose to be in harmony or disharmony with life.

For our own good—for the sake of our health, our comfort, our effectiveness in life—we must learn to forgive. If we don't, we will continue to be out of harmony with our body, our mind, our emotions, and the world about us. When we are willing to forgive, we open the floodgates of unconditional love and are once again in the flow of love and life!

Let the forces of light bring illumination to
humankind.
Let the spirit of peace be spread abroad.
May men and women of goodwill everywhere
meet in a spirit of cooperation.
May forgiveness on the part of all people be the
keynote at this time.
Let power attend the efforts of the great ones.
So let it be, and help us to do our part.

APPENDIX I

Psychosynthesis Workshops, Tapes, and Literature

1. Workshops on Unconditional Love and Forgiveness, led by Edith Stauffer, are available to groups. Contact Psychosynthesis International, below.

2. Teacher Training in the techniques and methods of Unconditional Love and Forgiveness are available to groups of ten or more. Contact Psychosynthesis International, below.

3. Tapes recorded by Edith Stauffer are available for sale. For information, send self-addressed stamped envelope to Psychosynthesis International, below.

4. For a list of available books and monographs on psychosynthesis topics, send a self-addressed stamped envelope to Psychosynthesis International, below.

Psychosynthesis International
Post Office Box 926
Diamond Springs, California 95619
Telephone: (916)622-9615

APPENDIX II

Psychosynthesis Organizations

UNITED STATES:
(Listed in ZIP Code Order)

The Synthesis Center
PO Box 575
Amherst, Massachusetts 01004

Berkshire Center for Psychosynthesis
PO Box 152, Hupi Road
Monterey, Massachusetts 01245

Psychosynthesis for the Helping Professional
PO Box 82
Concord, Massachusetts 01742

Synthesis Educational Foundation
236 Mystic Valley
Winchester, Massachusetts 01890

Psychosynthesis Center of New Hampshire
RFD 1, Box 680
Hancock, New Hampshire 03449

Maine Center for Psychosynthesis
338 Fore Street
Portland, Maine 04101

Vermont Center of Psychosynthesis
62 East Avenue
Burlington, Vermont 05401

Psychosynthesis Resource Center
111 Park Street, Suite 1-L
New Haven, Connecticut 06511

Psychosynthesis Institute of New York
5 Milligan Place
New York, New York 10011

The Psychosynthesis Center
PO Box 264, Eagle Farm Road
Uwchlan, Pennsylvania 19480

The Psychosynthesis Foundation of Florida, Inc.
164 Seaspray Avenue
Palm Beach, Florida 33480

Kentucky Center of Psychosynthesis
436 West 2nd Street
Lexington, Kentucky 40508

Psychosynthesis Institute of Minnesota
PO Box 8171
St. Paul, Minnesota 55108

Psychosynthesis Training and Counseling
9515 Provincial Lane
Wichita, Kansas 67212

Psychosynthesis Training and Counseling
1135 West Broadway
Newton, Kansas 67401

Eupsychia, Inc.
3930 West Bee Caves Road, Suite 6-B
Austin, Texas 78746

Intermountain Associates for Psychosynthesis
8508 Marquette NE 1
Albuquerque, New Mexico 87108

Psychosynthesis Training and Counseling
PO Box 50881
Pasadena, California 91105

International Association for
Managerial and Organizational Psychosynthesis
3308 Radcliffe Road
Thousand Oaks, California 91360

Psychosynthesis Training
PO Box 18185
San Francisco, California 94118

Psychosynthesis Training Program
718 Balboa Street
San Francisco, California 94118

Psychosynthesis Affiliates
17360 Melody Lane
Los Gatos, California 95030

Psychosynthesis Center of Sacramento
PO Box 161572
Sacramento, California 95816

Psychosynthesis Center
PO Box 152, 238 East Main Street
Ashland, Oregon 97520

High Point Northwest: A Psychosynthesis Center
23700 Edmonds Way
Edmonds, Washington 98020

Synthesis
PO Box 27181
Seattle, Washington 98125

CANADA:
(Listed in Postal Code Order)

Centre de Psychosynthesis du bas Saint Laurent
Escourt
Quebec G0L 1J0

Ecole de Psychosynthesis Roberto Assagioli
3432 rue Masson, Suite 200
Montreal, Quebec H1X 1R7

Psychosynthesis Pathways of Montreal
4816 Hutchison
Outremone, Montreal, Quebec H2V 4A3

Centre de Psychosyntheses de Montreal
433 est blvd St. Joseph
Montreal, Quebec H5J 1J6

Pigeon Hill Peacemaking Centre pour la paix
1965 Chemin St. Armand
Pigeon Hill, St. Armand, Quebec J0J 1T0

Toronto Centre for Psychosynthesis
263 Seaton Street
Toronto, Ontario M5A 2T5

SOUTH AMERICA

Asociación Argentina de Psicosíntesis y
Asociación Internacional de Ontosíntesis
Juncal 2061, P.1, Dto. B, Capital Federal
Buenos Aires 1116
Argentina

EUROPE:

The Trust for Psychosynthesis and Education
188-194 Old Street
London EC1 9BP
England

London Institute of Psychosynthesis
1 Cambridge Gate, Regents Park
London NW1 4JN
England

Greek Center of Psychosynthesis
Vas Sofias 98
11528 Athens
Greece

Instituut voor Psychosynthese
Kooikershof 7
5256 KD Heusden
Holland

Eckhart House, Institute of Psychosynthesis
19 Clyde Road
Dublin 4
Ireland

Centro Studi di Psicosintesi R. Assagioli
Piazza Modonna 7
Firenze 50123
Italia

SOUTH PACIFIC:

Psychosynthesis Training Centre of New South Wales
109 Oxford Street
Bondi Junction, New South Wales 2022
Australia

Psychosynthesis Training Centre of South Australia
3 Hoods Road
Northfield, South Australia 5085
Australia

Institute of Psychosynthesis
14 Dorset Street
Westmere, Auckland
New Zealand

Psychosynthesis Trust
1 Beach Road
Motueka, Nelson
New Zealand

NOTES

Foreword
1. Anderson, R.A., *Stress Power! How to Turn Tension into Energy,* (New York: Human Sciences Press, 1978).
2. Wolff, H.G., Wolff, S.G., and Goodell, H., *Stress and Disease,* (Springfield, Illinois: Charles C. Thomas, 1968).
3. Shekelle, R.B., et al, "Hostility, Risk of Coronary Artery Disease, and Mortality." *Psychosomatic Medicine,* 45:2, November 1983, pp. 109-114.

Chapter 1: Introduction
1. Concepts of the Essene *Code of Conduct,* rendered into English by Sadook de Mar Shimun, appear in *Enlightenment: Selected Passages from the Khaboris Manuscript,* (Atlanta, Georgia: Yonan Codex Foundation, 1974). Not yet published: Stauffer, Edith, *The Essenes and their Code of Conduct* (Burbank, California: Triangle Publishers, available 1987).
2. Roberto Assagioli, who originated psychosynthesis, wrote numerous monographs and is best known for his books, *Psychosynthesis: A Manual of Principles and Techniques,* (New York: Penguin Books, 1981) and *The Act of Will,* (New York: Penguin Books, 1974).
3. MacDougald, Dan: "Emotional Maturity Instruction", (Atlanta, Georgia: Yonan Codex Foundation).

Chapter 2: Naphsha: Our Connection with the Source
1. Assagioli, Roberto, *Psychosynthesis: A Manual of Principles and Techniques,* (New York: Penguin Books, 1981).
2. Shimun, Sadook de Mar, *Enlightenment: Selected Passages from the Khaboris Manuscript.* (Atlanta, Georgia: Yonan Codex Foundation, 1974).

Chapter 3: Attitudes: The Brain's Filters
1. Broorstein, Sylvia, "Notes on Right Speech as a Psychotherapeutic Technique," *Journal of Transpersonal Psychology,* 17:1, 1985.
2. Rahula, Walpola, *What the Buddha Taught,* (New

York: Grove Press, 1959). The passage quoted appeared in the Broorstein article cited above.

Chapter 7: The Second Attitude: The Attitude that Cures Mental Stress
1. Maltz, Maxwell, *Psycho-Cybernetics,* (New York: Prentice-Hall, 1960). The experiment was reported in *Research Quarterly* and subsequently described in Maltz's work.

Chapter 8: The Third Attitude: The Attitude of Humility
1. Hammarskjold, Dag, *Markings,* (New York: Alfred A. Knopf, Inc., 1964).

Chapter 16: Practicing Forgiveness
1. Goble, Frank, *Third Force Psychology: The Psychology of Abraham Maslow,* (New York: Washington Square Press, 1970).

Chapter 18: Prayer and Meditation
1. Roberto Assagioli, "Meditation", (San Francisco, California: Psychosynthesis Institute, 1973).
2. See Note 1, above.
3. See Note 1, above.
4. Eastcott, Michal J., *The Silent Path,* (York Beach, Maine: Samuel Weiser, Inc., 1969).
5. MacDougald, Dan, "Emotional Maturity Instruction" (Atlanta, Georgia: Yonan Codex Foundation).
6. Pelletier, Kenneth, *Mind as Healer, Mind as Slayer,* (New York: Dell Publishing Company, 1977).
7. LaShan, Lawrence, *How to Meditate,* (Boston, Massachusetts: Little, Brown & Company, 1974).
8. Assagioli, Roberto, "Meditation", (San Francisco, California: Psychosynthesis Institute, 1973).
9. See Note 8, above.
10. See Note 8, above.
11. See Note 8, above.
12. Parker, Robert, *Your Mind is Your Destiny,* (Newport Beach, California: Community Church of the Bay Newsletter, April/May 1978).

GLOSSARY

The terms listed here are either Aramaic words translated as closely as possible into English, or English words that are uncommon or have a particular meaning for the purposes of this book.

ABDEY: To produce, bear, or serve with effect.

ABILII: Regret for wrongs; sorrow. Deep desire for truth or to be "on target;" a willingness to correct mistakes and wrongs.

ALAHA: The Highest of the High, the Source of all.

ARAMAIC LANGUAGE: An ancient language dating back to the beginning of recorded history. Aramaic was the auxiliary language of the Persian empire, which stretched from the Mediterranean Sea to the Great Wall of China. It was the language of the Zoroastrian religion, of Abraham, of the Judeo-Christian faith, of Mohammed, and the Koran. Aramaic expresses transpersonal psychology so completely that it utilizes a syntax which portrays the working relationship between mind sets, perception, mind structures, reason, judgment, entities of the mind, human attitudes, and human behavior. It does not distinguish between the mental, physical, emotional, or spiritual, or between cause and effect.

ATTITUDE: A mind set (neural structure) which is a combination of feelings, thoughts, and memories that color our perceptions, life, and environment.

BELIEF SYSTEM: Facts, ideas, symbols, images, expectations, etc. which make up the attitudes one holds about oneself, others, and situations.

CONDITIONAL LOVE: Love which is based upon the meeting of certain demands, expectations, or conditions in order for it to be given.

DADCEAN: Complete, entire, whole, total, without blemish or fault.

DISCIPLINE: Use of reason and sensitivity to natural consequences in an effort to establish desirable goals and behavior.

DISEASE: The result of lack of harmony in an individual, due to the individual's blocking love and the flow of Naphsha's energy.

ESSENES: Members of an ancient sect, known for their ability to apply transpersonal qualities to their lives, thus creating a peaceful, effective, productive society. They recorded their rules for harmonious existence in the *Code of Conduct,* written in Aramaic, their native language.

FAILURE: Lack of achievement of a goal; the result of error; a means by which we learn.

FAITH: A judgment or conclusion that the Source and spiritual laws are valid.

FIRST LAW: See LAW OF ATTITUDES.

FORGIVE (SHBAG): To cancel demands and expectations one makes on the Source, others, and the self as a condition for expressing love and other positive attitudes.

GOAL: An objective or desire established and maintained by the will, controlling the selection of input data. A neural structure that determines what comes into the brain and what actions are taken.

GRATITUDE: A transpersonal quality which can change our attitudes and elevate our consciousness; a feeling of joyful appreciation for the good in self, others, and the environment.

GUILT: Negative and inharmonious feelings produced by unsound judgment and the belief that one has wrongfully failed to meet a demand placed by the Source, self, another, or a situation.

HEART-CENTER: Located in the center of the chest (not to be mistaken for the physical heart), it emits and distributes energy; a center of transmutation when it is open and functioning. It is directly related to the Naphsha.

HIGHER SELF: See NAPHSHA.

HOME IN RUKHA: See RUKHA.

HOSTILITY: An unsound attitude of hate and anger, causing us to be unaware of the good in a neighbor, the self, or the Source.

HUMILITY (MAKIKH): An attitude which enables us to see the needs of others as they see them or will see them, and a desire to fulfill those needs, if practical.

ILLNESS: See DISEASE.

INHIBITORY SYSTEM: That portion of the nervous system which filters stimuli entering into the brain in order to lower tension.

JUDGMENT: The mental act of comparison and discrimination by which knowledge of values and relations is mentally formulated; the power of arriving at a wise decision; the mind's process of incorporating sensory input, memory, and reason into a decision for action.

KENOOTA: Sound, proper, right, just, equitable, fair.

KHOOBA LOVE: An attitude of unconditional positive regard, causing one to become aware of what is good in others, self, or a situation. This attitude enables one to perceive what is fair and just.

LAW OF ATTITUDES: Sound principles regulating the course of our state of being, based on love for the Source, others, and the self.

LOVE: See CONDITIONAL LOVE; KHOOBA LOVE; RAKHMA LOVE; UNCONDITIONAL LOVE.

MALKOOTA D'SHMEYA: The way it ought to be; clean, sound, happy, desirable; a more perfect condition.

MASKEN: Home; place of mental, emotional, and physical rest.

MEDITATION: Reaching within and making contact with one's Naphsha, and beyond to the Source, in a search for truth and harmony with one's life, talents, abilities, opportunities, and for solutions to personal and global problems.

MIND SET: See ATTITUDE.

MOTIVATION: Tension produced by an existing and unachieved goal, resulting in movement toward carrying out the goal in order to relieve the tension.

NAPHSHA: Soul, Higher Self, essence, the "breath of life." Every person has a Naphsha, and is a Naphsha, by virtue of existence. Naphsha cannot be destroyed; it is the controlling core, the organizing center of energy, the managing agent, the source of mental, physical, emotional, and spiritual development. The Naphsha is the source of serenity, harmony, wisdom, forgiveness, and healing; it is in contact with universal laws and the laws of the individual's being.

NARTOUN: To gain love or material goods through one's ability to earn; to receive for service rendered.

NEIGHBOR: Anyone who is physically near and of whom one is mentally aware, including one's own Naphsha.

NITBEYOON: Cured of mental stress. There is no word or symbol in English to convey the idea of freedom from mental stress. Though inadequate, "comforted" is sometimes used.

PERSONAL SELF: The conscious, aware self which is the center of the personality and makes choices and decisions. It is the I with which we identify when we say, "I had a good day."

PRAYER: Reaching to the Source for truth to maintain one's mental home in Rukha and Naphsha, to keep before the mind the proper guidelines for growth; a petition seeking guidance and direction for our lives; an offering of thanksgiving or praise.

PUNISHMENT: Physical or emotional pain inflicted on self or another, stemming from behavior due to wrong attitudes.

RADPEAN: Harassment, insult, scorn by another.

RAKHMA LOVE: Love without demand, request,

reward, or return. Rakhma love is a universal love; it includes reason, thought, judgment, and action; it evolves from khooba love. See KHOOBA LOVE.

RAKHMANII: Love expressed without conditions.

RIGHT SPEECH: A choice of words which is positive and constructive, resulting in better relations with others and enhanced well-being within the speaker.

RUKHA: Spirit; an aspect of the Source which is available to the personal self and the Naphsha; an unseen force that operates on an exhalted or transpersonal level and is available to those who elevate themselves to that level of consciousness.

SELF: See HIGHER SELF; PERSONAL SELF; TRANS-PERSONAL SELF.

SHBAG: See FORGIVE.

SIN: An archery term for missing the mark.

SOURCE: The Creator; Author; Divine Authority; Essence of life; God; Divine Mind; the Highest Essence; the one in whom we live, move, and have our being.

SPIRITUAL: In its larger sense, describing any action which benefits humanity as a whole. It properly relates humans to one another and to the Source, and lifts that which is material toward the higher level of consciousness. Spiritual evolution is the unfolding of the latent divine potentialities within the individual Spiritual qualities cause us to love, desire to be loved, relate to others, and to grow, improve, and increase our effectiveness.

SUCCESS: Achievement of a goal.

TENSION: Disharmony occurring when the brain receives conflicting signals about a subject; the difference between the perceived level of stress and the ability of the individual to reduce it comfortably.

TOUVEYHOUN: Exalted dignity and function of the mind, desired by the Source of life for the well-being of all humans, rendering thoughts and actions which are in harmony with the will of the Source.

TRANSPERSONAL: Above and beyond the physical, emotional, and mental personality; a universal quality which regards humanity as a whole, for the purpose of expressing the good.

TRANSPERSONAL SELF: Higher Self, Naphsha, Soul; the Self that is above the personality. See TRANS-PERSONAL.

UNCONDITIONAL LOVE: Love for self, others, the Source, and inanimate objects which is given without demands, expectations, or conditions as a requisite for receiving the love.

WILL: The means by which the individual establishes and maintains goals and controls attitudes; that part of the self which makes choices and decisions, initiates action, and helps to fulfill goals.

SUGGESTED READING

The following works influenced the writing of this book, either as direct reference or as resource material. We offer this list with gratitude towards the authors and publishers, and as a guide to help you in your own pursuit of unconditional love and happiness.

Anderson, Robert A. *Stress Power! How to Turn Tension into Energy.* New York: Human Sciences Press, 1978.

Assagioli, Roberto. *The Act of Will.* New York: Penguin Books, 1974.

Assagioli, Roberto. "Meditation". San Francisco: Psychosynthesis Institute, 1973.

Assagioli, Roberto. *Psychosynthesis: A Manual of Principles and Techniques.* New York: Penguin Books, 1981.

Broorstein, Sylvia. "Notes on Right Speech as a Psychotherapeutic Technique". *Journal of Transpersonal Psychology* 17:1, 1985.

Eastcott, Michal J. *The Silent Path.* York Beach, Maine: Samuel Weiser, Inc., 1969.

Goble, Frank. *Third Force Psychology: The Psychology of Abraham Maslow.* New York: Washington Square Press, 1970.

Hammarskjold, Dag. *Markings.* New York: Alfred A. Knopf, Inc., 1964.

LaShan, Lawrence. *How to Meditate.* Boston: Little, Brown and Company, 1974.

MacDougald, Dan. "Emotional Maturity Instruction". Atlanta, Georgia: Yonan Codex Foundation.

Maltz, Maxwell. *Psycho-Cybernetics.* New York: Pocket Books, 1966.

Pelletier, Kenneth. *Mind as Healer, Mind as Slayer.* New York: Dell Publishing Company, 1977.

Rahula, Walpola. *What the Buddah Taught.* New York: Grove Press, 1959.

Shimun, Sadook de Mar. *Enlightenment: Selected Passages from the Khaboris Manuscript.* Atlanta, Georgia: Yonan Codex Foundation, 1974.

Edith R. Stauffer, Ph.D., is currently Director of Psychosynthesis International, which provides training for professionals around the world. In addition to her formal education, she has studied with Roberto Assagioli, M.D., the founder of psychosynthesis, at the Psychosynthesis Institute, Florence, Italy; the Martinus Institute, Copenhagen, Denmark; J.L. Moreno, M.D., Institute of Psychodrama and Group Therapy, New York; Dan MacDougald, Yonan Codex Foundation, Atlanta, Georgia; the American Institute of Family Relations, Los Angeles; Bula Williams, Ph.D., Southwest Counseling Service, Los Angeles; Fritz Kunkel, M.D., Los Angeles; and Brugh Joy, M.D., Southern California.

Dr. Stauffer served as Director of El Camino Counseling Service, Compton, California; and as Director of the Psychosynthesis Training Center of High Point Foundation, Pasadena, California.

She has taught at various campuses of both the University of California and California State University, and has served as consultant for numerous school districts throughout the United States.

In addition to writing course material, Dr. Stauffer has been invited to direct workshops for scores of professional and community organizations in various parts of the United States as well as Australia, Canada, Denmark, Holland, Italy, Japan, Korea, and New Zealand.

Married to Paul Stauffer for more than 55 years, Edith has two daughters and five grandchildren, all of whom continually receive her unconditional love—and forgiveness.